功包沙

I0418391

Shaolin Kung Fu Online Library

Authentic
Shaolin
Heritage

www.kungfulibrary.com

點
穴
術

Authentic Shaolin Heritage

DIAN XUE SHU

(DIM MAK)

Skill of Acting on Acupoints
2nd Edition

Translated from Chinese

First edition:

Tanjin, China, 1934

金
警
鐘

Jin Jing Zhong
Andrew Timofeevich (Translator)

Authentic Shaolin Heritage:

Dian Xue Shu (Dim Mak) - Skill of Acting on Acupoints (2nd Edition)

Editor of the translation Andrew Timofeevich. Translated by Wang Ke Ze, Leonid Serbin, Ekaterina Buga, Oleg Korshunov.

Shaolin Kung Fu Online Library

USA, 2024

ISBN: 979-8-9919633-3-6

shaolinkungfulibrary.com

First English Edition: USA, 2008

Disclaimer:

The author and publisher of this material are not responsible in any manner whatsoever for any injury whish may occur through reading or following the instruction in this manual. The activities, physical or otherwise, described in this material may be too strenuous or dangerous for some people, and the reader should consult a physician before engaging in them.

***

One must not use his Power for deception of people.

One must not rise over other people.

One must not use this Art for suppression of people.

If there are achievements, there should be flaws.

It is necessary to know about flaws to attain higher achievements.

It is necessary to breed the true greatness of Spirit.

Miao Xing

Contents

Part III: Symptoms and Consequences of Combat Impact on Points

Part IV: Training Methods for Fingers Hardening / From the book by Jin Jing Zhong "Training Methods of 72 Arts of Shaolin", Tanjin, 1934 /

***

Author's preface

I have no inclination to civil branches of science, I was always attracted by military path. In my childhood I often played war, attacked and took defense. When I read some war stories, I forgot about everything. Clothed in black, wearing high-boots, with a wooden sword on my back, I sat astride on a wooden bench and imagined that I was galloping on a horse back toward some noble feats. It was none other than manifestation of my nature. My ancestors were well-known people, they passed their Mastership from generation to generation, but after the decline of the monarchy[1] they gradually started to depart from this tradition. My ancestors realized that my nature was open to the Martial Arts, therefore they started to teach me in acrobatics and combat technique of Shaolin.

Editor's notes:
[1] The author means Qing dynasty (1644-1911) that ruled before Xinhai Revolution of 1911 in China.

When I grew up, I became a disciple of tutor Zhu Guan Peng who taught me the ancient style Tan Tui ("Kicking") and the technique of dislocation of bones and joints (Yu Gu). Tutor Zhu knew this method very well.

Then I was a disciple of tutor Yang De Shan and studied the Shaolin style Liu He Quan ("Fist of Six Harmonies"). The requirements were very strict and I had to do my best. Time, five years of training, passed quickly. During those years I trained myself when it was hot and when it was cold, did not stop lessons even at days-off and during holidays. I trained myself all the same, even if I was very busy in social activities. During those five years I managed to master four kinds of Gong Fu and gradually comprehended profound sense of the Martial Arts.

There were a lot of excellent masters, and I often thought about my further studies with the aim of deeper understanding of the Martial Arts. At that time I happened to meet tutor Yin De Kui. Then he was over 80 years old. In the past he roamed provinces of Shanxi, Shenxi, Hunan, Hubei, Sichuan, Guizhou, had popularity and good reputation. In his time he received inheritance from tutor Zhang, his skills were superb. I instantly understood that he was an excellent master and I became his apprentice with his permission. Senior disciple Guo Ze Yi replacing the tutor taught us skills. Sometime the tutor himself helped him and gave instructions to us. As Guo Ze Yi had already learnt from the tutor during 30 years, he mastered all that was the most valuable and reached perfection. That's why to learn from him meant the same as to learn from the very tutor. Our tutor was very good at "instinctive" Gong Fu, it is also called "supernatural" Gong Fu. This style differs from other schools, it rests upon the subconscious and uses hidden psychic forces, that's why it was called Xing Gong Quan – "The Fist of Subconscious Mastership". This Gong Fu has other names too: Ren Zu Men

("Teaching of Ancestors") and San Huan Men ("School of Three Emperors").

I, twenty years old lad, left civil service and fully devoted myself to military affairs, diligently worked as an instructor and trained myself in Kung Fu. Nevertheless, I often felt doubts. Fortunately, I met a lot of practiced people experienced in Kung Fu, a lot of like-minded persons. They helped and admonished me. I learnt many valuable things from them. In the mountains of Songshan I met His Reverend Miao Xing, the Head of the Shaolin Monastery, the living legend of that time. He liked my purposefulness and he started to teach me the style Luohan Quan, the 72 kinds of Shaolin Arts, methods of hitting acupoints and acupuncture (Dian Xue), technique of joint dislocation (Yu Gu), methods of grappling (Chin Na), and many other things.

I am grateful to my lucky star for being engaged in the Martial Arts for 21 years. I listened to admonitions of my Tutors and learnt a lot. I was born in a family of officials, but never had I a habit to enjoy respect and luxury, that's why I succeeded in getting good results. Moreover, I diligently learnt and all my tutors were well-known people. During whole my life I was engaged in the Martial Arts, I was taught, I did my best, all other pursuits were sacrificed to it. Was it done only to improve health or to become a tutor in Kung Fu and a hawker who sells a complex of movements (TAO)? Our Martial Arts are important means of strengthening the Nation and the State. Unfortunately, many Wu Shu masters put on airs and stagnated. They keep secrets from each other and don't share experience. It will be of no good. That's why we publish for the country all we have got and appeal for everybody to support our initiative and spread it. Let our Martial Art like the rising sun shines for the whole world, let our country be among powerful states. We collected all we had seen and heard, we gathered ancient manuscripts given to us by our tutors to compile the present book series. We hope that readers will make their comments that could be used to introduce corrections into the second possible editions.

Mad Jin Jing Zhong from the family of Yanjing.

Wrote it in the House of Dilapidated Books and Blunt Sword on the 1-st of March 23-th year of Chinese Republic (1934).

Foreword

DIAN XUE, a method of acting on acupoints, is very profound and extremely complicated kind of the Martial Art. In this book we endeavored to expound all we know about this kind of WU SHU as clearly and plainly as possible and give general information about it and its training methods. It is considered that it is impossible to fully acquire this method without well-known tutors. If WU SHU trainees want to acquire two or three wonderful kinds (styles) of the martial art, they need 20-30 years for that at least. It also takes 20-30 years of labor to educate a good doctor. One can imagine how it is complicated to simultaneously exercise in two kinds of GONG FU. Hard labor and determination are far from being enough. The key point was always availability of a competent tutor and his desire to pass over his mastery. But I wrote this book because I advocate the idea that a man who exercises the Martial Art should learn DIAN XUE too. You know, it will teach not only to defeat men but to help them too. Before learning to gain upper hand over men, it is necessary to perfectly learn how to cure and save them. However, it is necessary to have a great practical experience in order to perfectly acquire methods of curing and saving people. As saying goes: "If you save a lot of people, you will get a lot of the good for yourself."

Part I: Introduction

DIAN XUE SHU

Theoretical Fundamentals

The Martial Art has deep roots in history. When people of ancient times created the martial art, it was as natural as stars, mountains, and rivers around them. They took images of insects, monkeys and birds as a base and imitated their movements and habits. Everything developed step by step. When emperor Xuan Yuan invented weapons – sabers, swords, and pikes, it gave a rise to the martial art with the use of weapons. Over time training methods became more complicated and enriched. Various currents, trends, and schools appeared. Some acquired skills superficially, put up their skills for show, some learnt the essence of the teaching, highly valued and kept it in secret. Hundreds and thousands of years passed so. It is difficult to say now how training methods have changed as compared with ancient times.

Today, when we speak about the Martial Art, first of all we mean two main trends and four schools. The two main trends are SHAOLIN and WUDAN[2]. The four schools are SAN

Editor's notes:

[2] WUDAN - it means mountains of Wudan in the province of Hubei where one the Taoist centers in China, the birth-place of the so-called "Wudan" school of Martial Arts, is situated.

HUANG MEN – "School of Three Emperors", XIN YI MEN – "School of the Unity of Outer Form and Will", BA GUA MEN – "School of Eight Trigrams" and YAN MEN – "School of Yan". Historical investigations of the two trends and the four schools showed that SAN HUANG MEN has the most ancient history. The founder of SHAOLIN trend was Buddhist monk Da Mo (Bodhidharma) who came to China in the fall of the year DIN WEI (527 A.D.) in the reign of emperor Liang Wu Di. The founder of the WUDAN trend was Zhang San Feng[3]. He was born at the time of Song dynasty in the reign of emperor Hui Zong. The founder of SAN HUANG MEN was Ren Huang Shi. The founder of XIN YI MEN was Ji Jike[4]. The founder of BA GUA MEN was Dong Hai Chuan[5]. The founder of YAN MEN was Chen Zhou Yan. They are separated in time by hundreds and thousand years.

Each school and trend have their own advantages as regard to their content. As to their sources, their fundamentals belongs to Ren Huang Shi[6] and Huangdi[7]. The Chinese national heritage were preserved throughout years, introduced into practice and developed, it has not been lost until now. That is

---

Editor's notes:

[3] Zhang San Feng, Taoists wizard, supposedly lived in the XIII century.

[4] Ji Jike (1642 - 1697?), another name Ji Long Feng, also had a nickname "Wonderful Lance".

[5] Dong Hai Chuan (1813 – 1882), the founder of a style known in the West as BAGUA ZHANG – "Palm of Eight Trigrams".

[6] Ren Huang Shi, or Tien Huang Shi, one of the most ancient (mythological) rulers of China. It is said in "Historical Chronicles" by Sima Qian: "As soon as the Sky and the Earth were established, appeared Tien Huang Shi of twelve heads".

[7] Huangdi – Yellow Emperor; considered to be the first emperor of China and the ancestor of the Chinese nation; according to a legend, ruled during one hundred years up to 2450 B.C.

the contribution of the two schools and the four trends. All of them have weak and strong points. Now, when people say about WU SHU, they consider SHAOLIN the "external" school and WUDAN "internal" one. The main thing in the "external" school is hardness and in the "internal" school softness. Bur really SHAOLIN school also has "softness" and WUDAN school "hardness". When the difference between those schools is talked about, it resembles debates of scientists about nuances of differences in the teachings of Confucius[8] and Meng-Tse[9]. Also, they say that SAN HUANG is ancient secrets, YAN MEN is the summit of the Southern martial art, XIN YI is the skill of inner power, BAGUA is a teaching about "hardness" and "softness". The national heritage WU SHU includes the realization of nature of YIN and YANG, the teaching on the concord of "hardness" and "softness", the doctrine of victory over an enemy and education of people. Everything must be verified in practice, otherwise a moment will come when "hardness" driven to the utmost limit will break and "softness" will lose its base for development.

Editor's notes:

[8] Confucius, Kung-Tse (born about 551 – died in 479 B.C.), ancient Chinese thinker, founder of Confucianism. Was descended from an impoverished noble family and spent the most part of his life in the kingdom Lu (the territory of the modern province of Shandong). Was a small official in his young years, then founded the first private school in China. Main opinions of C. were expounded in his book "Talks and Opinions" ("Lun Yu") which is a record of sayings and talks of C. with his closest disciples and followers.

[9] Meng-Tse, teacher Meng, Mencius, Meng Ke, Zi Yu, Chinese thinker, the second after Confucius ("The Next after the Perfect Wise" – YA SHENG), one of the founders of Confucianism and forerunner of Neoconfucianism, author of the classic treatise of the same name, MENG-TSE, included into "the Thirteen Canons" (SHI SAN JING) and "The Four Books" (SI SHU) at the beginning of the II millennium B.C. (during the dynasty of Song).

72 kinds of Shaolin Martial Art are an evidence of effective practical application. In days of old there lived a well-known Shaolin monk Sun Tong from the state of LU[10]. He was very skinny, it seemed he even yielded to the wind and hardly was able to bear the weight of his dress. Once he was encircled by a dozen of strong lads. The monk joined his middle finger with the forefinger and made a movement toward the lads as if pointed a direction for somebody. Everybody around him were dumbfounded, it became hard for them to move and speak. Learned people understand that it is nothing else but the manifestation of DIAN XUE skill. The attackers started to kowtow before him and asked to teach them that skill. Sun replied: "I have been living in the Shaolin monastery more than 10 years and there I have learnt this trifling trade, but I may not pass it to anybody. You live in the country and you are not occupied with agriculture, you have learnt some leg and arm movements and think that you are masters of the Martial Art, your behavior is defiant. You are lucky that you have met me, otherwise you could be hard pressed". With these words he reanimated all of them. Those people got to know that DIAN XUE had come from Shaolin. Sun Tong himself was born in the town of Taian of the state of Lu. At first he mastered two kinds of martial art, NI ZONG and BAGUA, to perfection. Then he lived in the Shaolin monastery where he acquired the skill of DIAN XUE, methods of grappling CHIN NA, join dislocation methods YU GU and the skill "Iron Leg" from 72 Shaolin Arts. He was born at the time of dynasty QING, years of YONG JENG[11]. He was nicknamed "Sun Tong, Iron Leg". He was

---

Editor's notes:

[10] **LU, an ancient state of the epoch Zhou (XI – III centuries B.C.), birthplace of Confucius. Situated on the territory of the modern province of Shandong. This historical name was kept for that place and used during many centuries.**
[11] **Years of 1723-1736.**

also called "Almighty". Later he moved to Cangzhou. He passed down his mastery to Chen Shan. Chen Shan passed down his mastery to his son Chen Guang Zhi. Chen Guang Zhi passed down to his son Chen Yu Shan (he worked as the Chief Instructor in WU SHU at the office of the President[12]). Now the son of the latter can also teach that skill. Chen Shan also has disciples, one of them is Jiang Ting Ju. He passed down his mastery to Jiang Tai He. Jiang Tai He passed down to Jang Rong Qiao (at present he works as the editor-in-chief of the Central Palace of WU SHU, he founded "The Society of learning the Martial Art" in Shanghai). So up to our time there were sufficiently many men in the region of Cangzhou who mastered the art of DIAN XUE. The art of DIAN XUE is nothing else but GONG FU which is considered to be "soft". But in a combat it is a means for killing. It proves that "soft" GONG FU is inherent to Shaolin too.

The theory of the skill of DIAN XUE is very profound, training is accompanied by great difficulties. Besides, all who have acquired that skill to some extend keep it in secret from each other, therefore there are very few men who are in command of that GONG FU perfectly. Even the people who exercise WU SHU know only names of masters of that GONG FU but do not know training methods. It is very pity because that method can be used not only as a method to subdue people, it is in close connection with medicine, acupuncture in particular. That method can save men's life at critical moments. The theory of acupuncture is very complicated, it should be thoroughly studied. That concerns not only the people of strong physical build.

Editor's notes:

[12]It means Sun Yat Sen (his other names: Sun Zhong Shan, Sun Wen) (1866 - 1925), the first (provisional) president of the Chinese Republic (1 January - 1 April, 1912).

The human body is considered to be a part of TAI JI[13], the universal source of life which basically consists of YIN and YANG. Interaction between YIN and YANG give birth to WU XING[14], "Five Elements"; their combinations bring about life, death, and development. The man lives only thanks to QI and blood. If QI and blood are harmonized, life blooms. If QI and blood are not in harmony, there is a possibility of an illness and death. As far as healthy people are concerned, sometimes body damage can lead to disproportion between QI and blood and that is fraught with death. It is possible to restore the harmony by using the skill of DIAN XUE. Generally speaking, QI and blood are the source of life, they are in a continuous circulation through certain channels of the body depending on time of the day. There are 12 channels, 4 main vessels, 2 heel vessels, 2 connecting vessels and 365 acupoints in the human body. Passage of QI and blood in channels do not coincide in time, they are divided into 12 phases of SHI CHEN[15]. At a particular time the main stream of QI and blood concentrates in a particular channel and fills particular points. There are rules of filling points[16] depending on time of the day: time ZI SHI (from 11 p.m. to 1 a.m.) - point REN ZHONG; time CHOU SHI (from 1 a.m. to 3 a.m.) - point TIAN TING; time YIN SHI (from 3 a.m. to 5 a.m.) - point QI KONG; time MOU SHI (from 5 a.m. to 7 a.m.) – point DA ZHU; time CHE SHI (from 7 a.m. to 9 a.m.) - point TAI YANG (temple); time SI SHI (from 9 a.m. to 11 a.m.) –

Editor's notes:

[13] TAI JI, "The Great Bound", the foundation of the universe, the beginning and the source of all that exist in Chinese traditional philosophy.

[14] WU XING, "FIVE ELEMENTS", a system of five primary elements – metal, wood, water, fire, and earth.

[15] SHI CHEN, a unit of time equal to 1/12 of a day, i.e. two hours; the count begins from 11 p.m.

[16] Localization of points, rules and methods of pressing and hitting them are given in the main part of the book.

point SHANG CANG; time WU SHI (from 11 a.m. to 1 p.m.) – point MEI WAN; time WEI SHI (from 1 p.m. to 3 p.m.) - point QI KAN; time SHEN SHI (from 3 p.m. to 5 p.m.) – point DAN TIEN; time YOU SHI (from 5 p.m. to 7 p.m.) - point BAI HAI; time XU SHI (from 7 p.m. to 9 p.m.) - point XIA YIN; time HAI SHI (from 9 p.m. to 11 p.m.) - point YONG QUAN.

If we know it, we can determine the localization of the main QI and blood flow for any time of a day. Then we use the method DIAN XUE to act on a "filled" point and it results in "closing" the point. Thus, the channel through which QI and blood circulate is blocked. As a result of it extremities grow numb and weak, they can not move, a man even can not speak. In order to open "closed" points and restore the flow of QI and blood, it is necessary to act on the respective points. Otherwise it will be difficult to restore the initial state.

There are 12 channels, 4 main vessels, 2 heel vessels, and 2 connecting vessels in the human body. All points of the human body are situated along those channels. Moreover, there are especially important points. Points can be "big", "small", "living", and "dead". Total number of "big" points is 108, including 72 points which cause if affected numbing (paralysis) of extremities, 36 "points of death", 271 "small" points, 72 points causing faint (loss of consciousness). There are points which cause, if being acted on, dumbness or atrophy (temporary loss of physical strength). Although it is not fatal, but it leads to temporary loss of enemy's ability to resist. After all, DIAN XUE SHU is not too difficult science.

Now the people who practice Martial Arts know that there is such a kind of WU SHU, but they do not know the training methods. However, it does not mean that this kind of WU SHU is difficult. The matter is that practitioners of martial arts are out for external manifestation, forgetting about the essence, or tutors make no progress, stew in their own juice. It seems to an outsider that the meaning of exercising in martial arts is to become stronger than others, but actually the essence is strengthening health and spirit in order to be physically strong men and live for a long time, be able to protect themselves. Therefore, ancient noble men said that practitioners of martial arts had to make the main stress on morals and virtue rather than to physical strength. Physical strength can make a man obey but he is far from being sincere when he does it. However, a virtual man of high morals, in spite of his physical strength being inferior compared with others, wins respect. It is just the morals of the martial art. They say that who is able of killing must be able of saving. The man who perfectly acquired this Gong Fu has only to raise a hand and the enemy immediately feels fatal danger. But on the other hand, he is able to reanimate a dying man.

If you can only kill and can not save (reanimate), it is called "deadly hand". It is unacceptable. It is necessary first to learn to save people before acquiring the martial art. It is the art of DIAN XUE that is the most suitable method for that. But injuring people, blocking channels and blood vessels can be done with the same method. Later I read the work "Secrets of curing body damages" written by tutor Yin De Kui. It says that it is not difficult to cure body damages but it is difficult to select points, the same is with medicines: it is not difficult to use them but it is difficult to determine them. In order to cure a body damage, it is necessary first to locate it, determine its nature and points to be influenced and only than to decide which method should be used – surgery or drug medication. It is necessary to succeed in that skillful hands would restore people's health and drugs you prescribe cure diseases. Otherwise as a result of your wrong actions or drugs mistakenly prescribed, you will not save a sick man, on the contrary, they will finish him. So they say, irrespective of your wish to win or save people, you may not know all other methods, but you must know the art of DIAN XUE and YU GU methods of joint dislocation. At that the art of DIAN XUE has priority over the YU GU methods of joint dislocation.

The DIAN XUE technique has been developing since ancient time and many people knew it. However, this GONG FU is almost lost now due to selfishness of people. At present most specialists in this sphere of WU SHU belong to the category of "deadly hand". They perfectly acquired methods of defense and attack but ignore a method of saving men. Even those who advertise their abilities in curing body damages know little about the structure of a man's skeleton and have only a small set of ready-made medicines. They can not know all details of the art of DIAN XUE.

I also exercised a martial art and trained myself at home in my young days[17]. When I got a little older, I learnt under the guidance of several masters. At my spare time I read a lot. Once I found a hand-written book "Secrets of the Art of DIAN XUE". That book was copied by Ong Gui, one of my ancestors. Later my tutor Zhu Guan Peng presented me with the book "Cannons of a Fist Combat", also hand-written, one of its articles was "Deadly DIAN XUE". The article described in detail 36 points used in the practical DIAN XUE. I did not learn that method thoroughly enough, therefore I did not reach perfection in its practical application. I also read the treatise "Teaching on Fist of Eight Trigrams" written by

---

Editor's notes:

[17] The author of the book is a descendant of a noble family Yan Jing. He wrote in the preface for his other book "Training Methods of 72 Arts of Shaolin": "My ancestors were well-known people, they passed their Mastership from generation to generation..." /See for detail: www.kungfulibrary.com/.

master Sun Lu Tang[18], it also said about the art of DIAN XUE. But my poor knowledge did not permit me to understand all secrets of those methods. When I visited the province of Henan as a gust, I heard that there was the wonderful master Liu Hui. He had mastered the methods of "YIN of Eight Trigrams" and "YANG of Eight Trigrams". "YIN of Eight Trigrams" is composed of 72 "old" and 64 "young" tendons. Besides, the style of "Eight Trigrams" (BA GUA) includes several "hard" methods. The uncle of my best friend, Sun Ci Chang, is in command of that method. I also read the work "Lectures on Taiji Quan" written by the honorable Chen Pin San. In his lectures he also says that besides QI GONG he exercises DIAN XUE. I also read some books of the WU DAN school and got to know that the method DIAN XUE is included into the Shaolin Taizu Quan where 9 "points of death", 9 "points of faint", 9 "points of paralysis", and 9 "points of dumbness" are acted on. Four by nine is total 36. All that proves that the art of DIAN XUE does not belong to only one of any schools or styles. Each school has it own secrets. When I lived in the temple of Shaolin, my tutor Miao Xing[19], a dean of the Shaolin monastery, passed down to me the art of Dian Xue Shu and secret book "Training Methods of 72 Arts of Shaolin"[20]. I preserved everything. But I am sorry to say that I am a little dull from birth, so I could not realize the profundity of the

---

Editor's notes:

[18] Sun Lu Tang (1861—1933), famous master of classic Taoist schools of the martial art, author of several works on the theory of the martial arts.

[19] For detail see: Jin Jing Zhong. Training Methods of 72 Arts of Shaolin. /www.kungfulibrary.com/

[20] At present the book "Training Methods of 72 Arts of Shaolin" has been translated into English and published in electronic format on our site. You can order this book here: www.kungfulibrary.com.

method[21]. I trained myself under the guidance of Guo Je Pu, an older disciple. My tutor Yin De Kui was also trained at Shaolin. He is well-known in five northern provinces of China. He is one of the best disciples of master Zhang Luo Zhong. Guo siansheng[22] showed me a book "Cannons of San Hong Men Fist" hand-written by Zhang Luo Zhong. It contains the chapter "Rules of application of DIAN XUE SHU". He explained to me in detail the contents of that book. As I have poor memory, I wrote everything that Guo siansheng told me.

I wish all DIAN XUE practitioners to lay stress on morals rather than on force. From one hand, employing the art of DIAN XUE, it is possible to withstand hostile attacks, use it for self-defense and avoid a lot of troubles. From the other hand, with that method people can be cured and saved. If you have force and display unbridled license, you will only injure people, only kill and not save them. So you can be up to a lot of troubles. Such actions not only break the law, they will be punished by the Almighty as well. That is the road to death. It is a wrong choice.

We told you about sources and importance of the art of DIAN XUE. As for the training techniques, they will be expounded below.

Editor's notes:

[21] A standard pejorative phrase said by all Chinese masters who follow the tradition. The Code of Martial Virtue WU DE specifies to a speaker to belittle his merits and praise merits of a tutor.

[22] Siansheng, a polite form of naming an older person in China; used as a title corresponding to Mr. or Sir, lit "teacher".

Summarizing Article

It is permissible to act on acupoints in order to harm (damage) a man only for the sake of a just matter. Sometimes one can not help using it, for instance, if you face a strong enemy who intends to maim or even kill you. In that case, if you don't react in due manner, it will mean the same as if you are waiting for execution with arms tied. However, one can act rightfully or unrightfully in such a situation, it is often enough just to weaken (neutralize) the villain to eliminate the danger.

Treatment for different diseases is the primary and the most important duty of the art of acting on acupoints. If I wounded a man or damaged some point belonging to a certain channel, I must know on which point and how I should manually act or what medicine I should use in order to cure a damage or disease. It is the unshakable law. If a disciple is eager to learn only methods of defeating the enemy, it is a one-sided way. It does not matter if we consider methods of suppressing the enemy or methods of saving the man, in any case general (base) training is needed. It is necessary to begin acquiring the skill at the very beginning and get ingenuity in its employment. You must know names and location of acupoints so that you can stretch your arm and touch the required point at once, finding its location unmistakably and precisely. Otherwise you would look like a child who sees a tripod and knows that it is a tripod, sees a water pool and knows that it is a water pool but can not raise the tripod or cross the water pool.

In connection with the above, the art of acting on points DIAN XUE SHU requires good technical preparedness and high mental qualities. Besides these requirements, however, it is necessary to perfect knowledge of meridians (channels) JING[23], starting from acquiring skills through explanations (to the text). One must learn to find points at a glance, find channels, then the disciple will have mastery in the martial art. But this technique must not be learnt at random, it is necessary to avoid chaotic character of learning, it can only make hindrance and take away. In that case a trainee engaging the enemy tries to employ this kind of GONG FU as ordinary (common) techniques done in a combat. Arm blows, kicking, retreats and attacks – they are usual GONG FU that can not withstand deadly QI moving with a drone and penetrating acupoints. The knowledge of the localization (of the main stream) of QI (is important) in the DIAN XUE technique. Later, after returning to a quiet state of purity and modesty, you will laugh at those who abandoned (the principles) and stubborn men. Because there are great differences in that matter, especially in training methods. In a word, punching and kicking are outer manifestation of GONG FU. A man who learns DIAN XUE practices "close", or actual "internal" GONG FU. But not every man is capable of succeeding in this knowledge, not every man can be trained.

Before teaching a man the technique, it is certainly necessary first to understand if that man suits for learning it or not. The technique should not be taught in the same manner as common pugilistic methods (QUAN FA) which disciples learn. If a man has great abilities, strong and uncompromising nature, even though he is short and the strength of his arms is not enough even for tying a hen, he will certainly succeed in

---

Editor's notes:

[23] Hieroglyph JING means "channels", or "meridians" of a human body and scrolls of sacred texts as well.

obtaining high results in the art. If he is brave and courageous and his strength is enough to raise a big tripod, he will also can not help advancing in this art. Moreover, if he has some knowledge of medicine (acupuncture and cauterization), it would much easier to make progress in the acquisition of this skill.

We want you to understand that the art of acting on acupoints DIAN XUE SHU is many-sided, its depth is bottomless, the methods of mastering it are diverse. Therefore, an extremely small number of people advanced in acquiring this skill in the old times and at present.

The writer of these lines received the Secret Teaching from his Tutor, he is sorry that now no pureness exists in hearts of those who learn this Art. There are three levels and nine stages in training the technique which must be acquired successively.

36 Main ("Deadly") Points in DIAN XUE SHU

There are many aqupoints on the human body, but 36 main points are distinguished in the DIAN XUE skill. Being acted on them, the life of a man is in danger. A man who has been injured so yields to treatment with difficulty. That's why people who are in command of the DIAN XUE skill try to avoid acting on those 36 points. Masters of this GONG FU know that those are "deadly" and "faint-causing " points[24], the impact can be light and strong. All 36 points mentioned below are deadly, a man can not be saved if they were strongly affected. They differ in that from "faint-causing" points. Although, when "faint-causing" points are acted on, a man faints, he can be reanimated.

Below are given names of those 36 points and figures showing their location on the human body.

Editor's notes:

[24] That is, impact on these points causes death ("deadly points") or faint ("faint-causing points").

Names of 36 Deadly Points

1 – BAI HUI XUE

2 – TAI YANG XUE

3 – BI LIANG XUE

4 – REN ZHONG XUE

5 – YA SAI XUE

6 – KAI KONG XUE

7 – TIAN JING XUE

8 – JIAN YUAN XUE

9 – QI MENG XUE

10 – XUAN JI XUE

11 – JIANG TAI XUE

12 – QI MEN XUE

13 – QI KAN XUE

14 – ZHANG MEN XUE

15 – DAN TIAN XUE

16 – XIA YIN XUE

17 – BAI HAI XUE

18 – QU CHI XUE

19 – MAI WAN XUE

20 – SAN YIN JIAO XUE

21 – YANG CHONG XUE

22 – TAI XI XUE

23 – TAI CHONG XUE

24 – YONG QUAN XUE

25 – TIAN GU XUE

26 – DUI KOU XUE

27 FEN YAN XUE

28 – GUA BANG XUE

29 – FEN HUANG RU DONG

30 – JI LIANG XUE

31 – FEN WEI XUE

32 – JI XIN XUE

33 – JING CU XUE

34 – XIAO YAO XUE

35 – QIAO KAO XUE

36 – HUAI GU XUE

解 圖 面 正

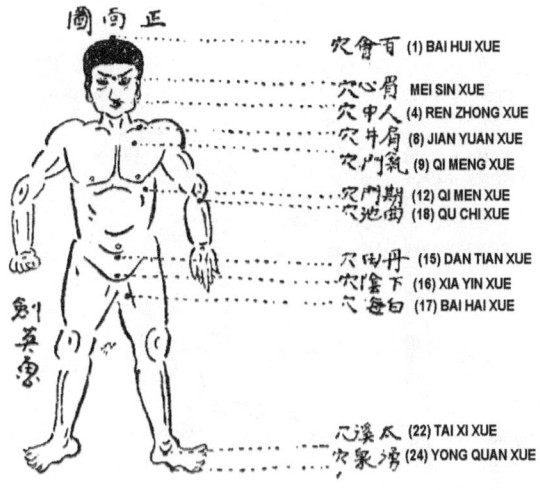

正面圖

穴會百 (1) BAI HUI XUE
穴心眉 MEI SIN XUE
穴中人 (4) REN ZHONG XUE
穴井肩 (8) JIAN YUAN XUE
穴門氣 (9) QI MENG XUE
穴門期 (12) QI MEN XUE
穴池曲 (18) QU CHI XUE
穴田丹 (15) DAN TIAN XUE
穴陰下 (16) XIA YIN XUE
穴海白 (17) BAI HAI XUE
穴溪瓦 (22) TAI XI XUE
穴泉湧 (24) YONG QUAN XUE

Fig.1
Front View

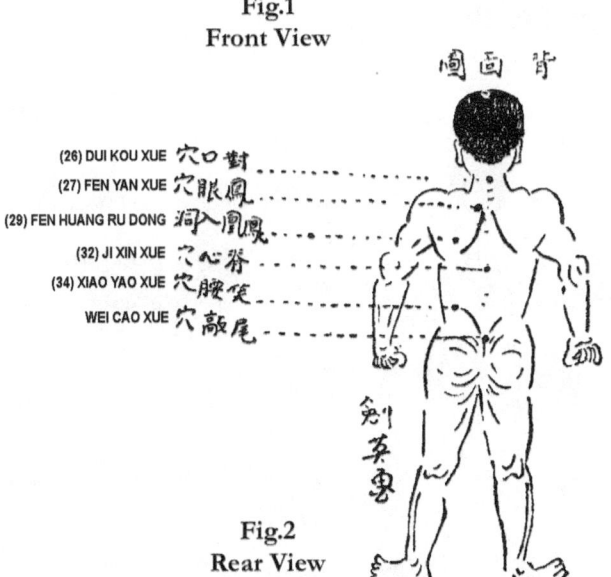

背面圖

(26) DUI KOU XUE 穴口對
(27) FEN YAN XUE 穴眼鳳
(29) FEN HUANG RU DONG 洞入鳳鳳
(32) JI XIN XUE 穴心脊
(34) XIAO YAO XUE 穴腰笑
WEI CAO XUE 穴敲尾

Fig.2
Rear View

背 面 圖 解

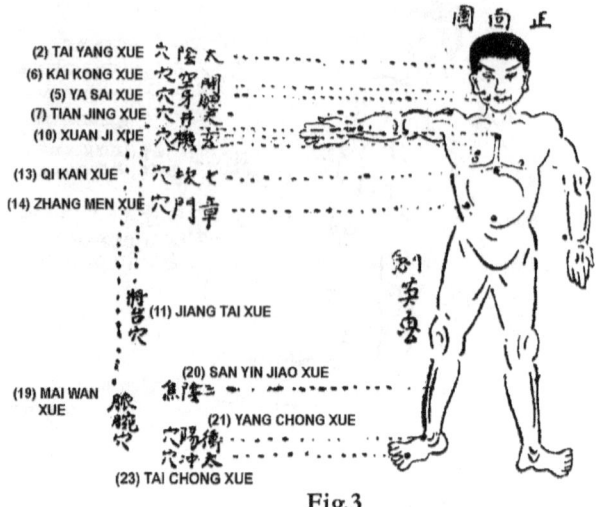

正 面 圖

(2) TAI YANG XUE — 太陽穴
(6) KAI KONG XUE — 開腔穴
(5) YA SAI XUE — 牙腮穴
(7) TIAN JING XUE — 天井穴
(10) XUAN JI XUE — 璇璣穴

(13) QI KAN XUE — 七坎穴
(14) ZHANG MEN XUE — 章門穴

(11) JIANG TAI XUE — 將台穴

(20) SAN YIN JIAO XUE — 三陰交
(19) MAI WAN XUE — 脈腕穴
(21) YANG CHONG XUE — 陽衝穴
太冲穴
(23) TAI CHONG XUE

Fig.3
Front View

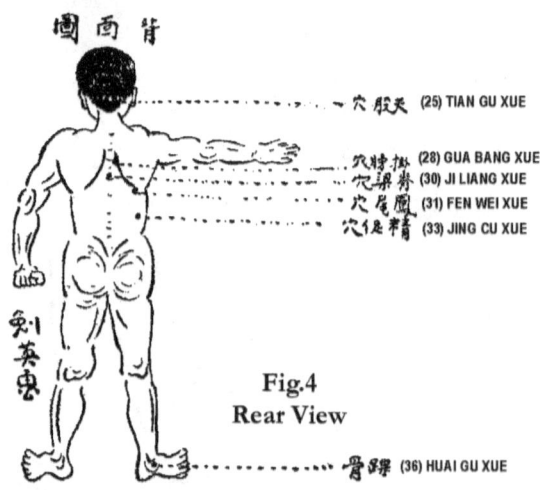

背 面 圖

天股穴 (25) TIAN GU XUE

拱膊穴 (28) GUA BANG XUE
脊梁穴 (30) JI LIANG XUE
鳳尾穴 (31) FEN WEI XUE
精促穴 (33) JING CU XUE

Fig.4
Rear View

踝骨 (36) HUAI GU XUE

正 面 圖 解

點穴術中最實用之十二四穴

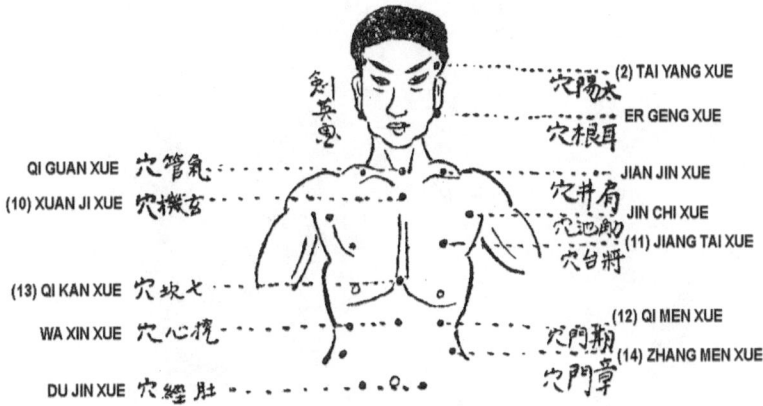

穴陽太 (2) TAI YANG XUE
穴根耳 ER GENG XUE

QI GUAN XUE 穴管氣
(10) XUAN JI XUE 穴機玄

穴肩井 JIAN JIN XUE
穴肩井 JIN CHI XUE
穴池勁 (11) JIANG TAI XUE
穴台將

(13) QI KAN XUE 穴坎七
WA XIN XUE 穴心挖

穴門翔 (12) QI MEN XUE
穴門章 (14) ZHANG MEN XUE

DU JIN XUE 穴經肚

Fig.5
Front View
24 points the most
often used in DIAN XUE SHU

點穴術中最易致命之十三穴

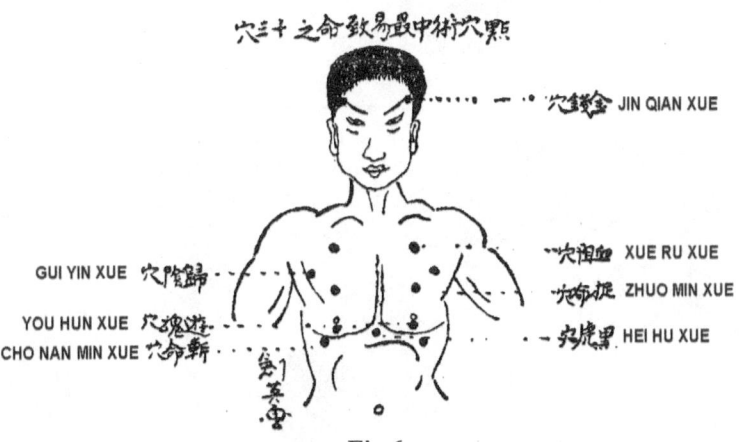

穴錢金 JIN QIAN XUE

GUI YIN XUE 穴陰歸

穴潤血 XUE RU XUE
穴敏捉 ZHUO MIN XUE

YOU HUN XUE 穴魂遊
CHO NAN MIN XUE 穴命斬

穴虎黑 HEI HU XUE

Fig.6
Rear View
13 the most dangerous deadly points used in
DIAN XUE SHU

Part II: Three Levels of Mastery, Nine Stages of Training

THE FIRST LEVEL OF MASTERY

The First Stage of Training. Familiarization With Points

The main thing in DIAN XUE SHU is the knowledge of point location. Knowing the location of points and their "fullness" (activity) at different time of the day, you may make a movement toward those points with your hand and get an effect. Otherwise you will be like a blind man, everything will fail. That's why the most important at the beginning is to learn the location of points. It is necessary not only to say where certain points are located, but unmistakably palpate their location with eyes closed. The training method is as follows: it is necessary first to fix in mind names of points of a certain channel and then their location. All points of the channel should be marked on a wooden dummy. Look straight at the beginning, later askance[25], then in darkness and show those points. When you learn to do so without mistakes, the work with this channel will be over. Then, work in the same manner with the second, third one and so on up to the twelfth channel. After that, you have to work with points of four main vessels, two heel vessels QIAO and two connecting vessels WEI, at last with all points at once. It is necessary to attain a flawless level, without any mistake. It should be taken into account that each point occupies very little place, therefore the least deviation is not permissible. Ignorant people may think that familiarization with points is not very difficult matter. But actually, it is not so easy, because each point occupies not more than 2 or 3 FEN[26] all in all. If you wish to subdue somebody, you may fail, if you wish to cure somebody, you may also fail. You can even do irremediable harm. Therefore, it is necessary to learn points and their location in DIAN XUE SHU very thoroughly. It will be easier later provided you have acquired the first stage thoroughly. But it will take one year of training at least.

Editor's notes:

[25] The employment of peripheral vision is meant here.
[26] 1 FEN is equal to 0.33 cm.

The Second Stage of Training. Search for Channels

What is called as points of acupuncture is not simply certain spots on a human body. They are the points that must be known and distinguished, and not "empty" spots without an access for QI and blood (at a given moment) or those points and channels where QI and blood have already passed. If, for instance, a point is "empty", it is impossible to attain the required effect with the method, much as one should like, even though fingers have a knack and mastery. It is possible to attain the required result only if QI and blood are present at the point. In that case it shines like a sea pearl and it can be found – one among a lot of other points. QI and blood reach a (certain) spot in certain time intervals, QI and blood move through channels along the exact route. The 12-hour period embraces 12 channels and the points connected with those 12 channels. That's why, when learning DIAN XUE SHU, besides the knowledge of points, their connection with channels, and their location, it is necessary to know channels through which QI flows and channels (arteries) through which blood moves in a human body. A doctor must unmistakably determine in which time interval QI and blood reach a certain point and at what time it passes without reaching a certain spot, and must not make a slightest mistake at that.

If you know about changes in point activities by time, you can act on active points and cause their damage, which will lead to a delay (stopping) of the movement of QI and blood. If normal movement (of QI and blood) is impossible, or moreover, a channel is obstructed, a man can lose consciousness or fall into a bad state of health. Methods of point acting can restore the initial state, but to do that, one must know Chinese medicine, be able to use acupuncture and cauterization and have adequate attestation. It is high time to say shortly that it is impossible to determine all meridians (channels) hidden in a human body and exactly locate them. However, it is necessary to know principal points and channels and understand the essence. Other "small" points have not been elaborated and described. It is necessary to do one's utmost in the process of learning to acquire that skill. It is quite possible to reach this stage of mastery during one year if you devote enough time to it.

It is important to distinguish time intervals in a full annual cycle as well, it should be also taken into account. The Earth makes a complete revolution (around the Sun) for 365 days and it is connected to points on a human body. If you base yourself on certain principles and develop in yourself the ability to conform with them, there will be progress in your mastery. If the main stream of QI and blood reached a certain spot at some time, it means energy is available at this point. If that time has not yet come or that time has already passed, the main stream of QI and blood does not reach (this point) and, therefore, it is difficult to get the result. Only observing all necessary conditions, after reaching a certain level of mastery and accumulating practical experience in addition, you will be able to act according your own intentions and gain a full victory over your enemy with the help of a sudden method. Otherwise you will make mistakes "before", "after", "more to the left", "more to the right" type and it will be impossible to gain perfect mastery[27].

Blood circulation is governed by a certain time law that must be known, 12 principal channels of a human body are active at a certain time, it must be well comprehended. That's why the stage "search for channels" also includes learning laws of QI and blood movement through those channels. Thus, the study of "external" and "internal" aspects of the problem is interconnected, it should be brought into concord with the point study. Actually, it is very difficult to learn and comprehend, both approaches must be united in a single course of practice without breaking the prescribed procedure of learning. In such a way great success can be attained in mastery and effective employment of the technique can be achieved in practice.

Certainly, "search for channels" is a separate stage, it can be practiced without deep penetration into the theory. However, ancient treatises on DIAN XUE SHU, directions on 12-hour cycles and the location of principal points, 12 channels of QI and blood circulation in the form of songs say about the necessity for the profound study of laws of circulation. As to the practical employment of laws of circulation, the knowledge of point activity at certain time allows to clearly realize the situation and perform purposeful and effective actions. It is impossible to fail under such conditions!

Editor's notes:

[27] Time mistakes when the main stream of QI and blood has not reached yet or, on the contrary, passed the point to be acted and mistakes in space accuracy in point impact are meant here.

The Third Stage of Training. How to Put Questions

If a man who learns DIAN XUE SHU thinks that he already knows all points and channels, anyhow he must be often examined to avoid mistakes. Best of all, a specialist in DIAN XUE SHU can do it by asking, for instance, such questions as "Where is such-and-such point?" or pointing at a spot and asking "What point is it?" It is necessary to ask about the principal points at first, then about points of minor importance. Later, it is necessary to ask pell-mell, unsystematically. If he who is examined always answers correctly, he may be asked about some certain channels and blood vessels and their connection with internal organs. Later, he must be asked about blood and QI circulation: at which time of the day and where is the main QI and blood flow? When (time of the day) and on which points must one act to damage certain channels, blood vessels (arteries), and internal organs? Which symptoms are noticed in a victim, which method and which medicine can revive him? And so day after day one can get great success with small efforts. A good teacher often does in such a way: he quotes several phrases from some known literary work, asks his pupils the source of citation and proposes them to continue citing. If you know bad, you can not answer at once. That method helps to fix in mind learning aids. The same is with DIAN XUE SHU. Only in this case a man who asks must be a professional, a specialist in acupuncture. If he is an amateur and knows only the names of points, he will not be able to say if an answer is right or not. It is a good thing if the answer is right, but what about a wrong answer? In that case irremediable harm can be inflicted on people.

It is necessary to pay special attention to learning "deadly" and "difficult" points. Deadly points are the points, being strongly acted on, a man can not be saved; difficult points are the points located at spots which are difficult to access, for example, in joints or in a thick layer of muscles. To act on "deadly" points means to take somebody's life. It is immoral. If you act on "difficult" points with insufficient technique or with a weak impact, you can not stop QI and blood flow. Therefore, it is necessary to pay the most serious attention to training. You should be a well-trained man to proportion (to control) precisely the force of impact on "deadly" points, you must not abuse it. "Difficult" points are just the other way about, they need a certain, often significant effort in order to get effect.

The above three stages (steps) of training make up the first level of mastery (GONG FU) in the skill DIAN XUE. After their acquirement one can proceed to training in the second level of GONG FU.

THE SECOND LEVEL OF MASTERY

The Fourth Training Stage. Finger Hardening

The whole innermost essence of DIAN XUE SHU – "Skill of touching acupuncture points" lies in the force of the only finger. In order to win an enemy, physical force can be employed and fists and legs used. But the force of one finger is limited very much. Furthermore, collision of fingers with a hard surface can cause a body damage. Therefore to suppress people with a finger is a rather 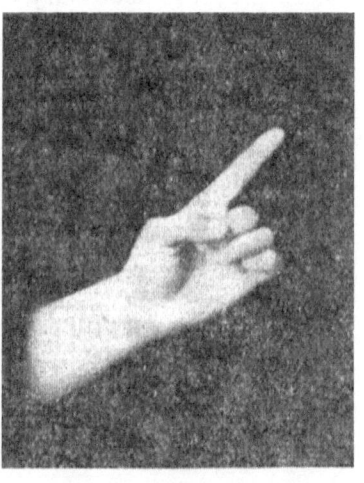 complicated matter. You must be in command of a great skill for it, otherwise you can not reach what you wish. Consequently, those learning DIAN XUE must first of all acquire all training methods which were expounded in the above section "Three stages of the first level of GONG FU". Only in that case finger training will make sense.

There are various and diverse training methods for fingers. It is necessary to choose one or several methods and systematically adhere to it (or them). Finger training can be done either successively or simultaneously with other required exercises. Any selection can be done. We shall mention some of methods for you to select conveniently. For instance, there are in 72 Shaolin Arts[28] such wonderful exercises as "Diamond finger", "Piercing through stones", "Rubbing palms", "Cinnabar palm", "Rubbing and thrusts", "Jumping centipede", or "The skill of slithering snake", and etc[29]. A board of spruce can be also used for training. The middle and forefinger are to be trained, or only forefinger. It is necessary to touch the board of spruce with a finger tip, at first slightly, then stronger and stronger. Three months later, the finger tip becomes noticeably harder as compared with its state at the beginning of training. At that time change the board with a brick. After

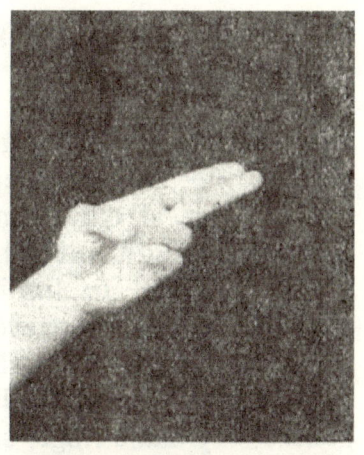

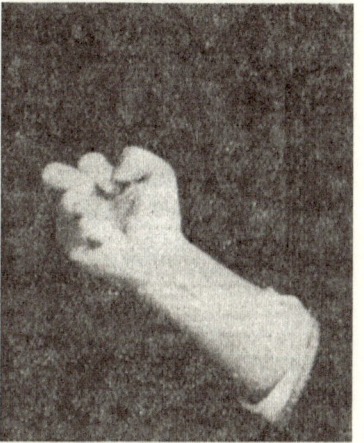

Editor's notes:

[28] See for detail: Jin Jing Zhong. Training Methods of 72 Arts of Shaolin. Tanjin, 1934. You can order this book here: www.kungfulibrary.com.

[29] See Chapter 4: "Training Methods for Fingers Hardening".

another three months change the brick for a stone. And so is day in and day out.

After one year the finger is thought to be sufficiently trained. But if you continue training, the result will be better. It is possible to inflict a significant body damage by using this GONG FU. That is so-called "outer" GONG FU. It is necessary that a finger should touch acupuncture points. Achievement of such level demands hard training during a year at least. If you wish to achieve the same effect without touching a human body, i.e. acquire "inner" GONG FU (QI GONG), it is more difficult. It must be taken into consideration that training according "Diamond finger", "Piercing through stones", "Rubbing palms", "Cinnabar palm", "Rubbing and thrusts", "Jumping centipede", or "The skill of slithering snake" and other methods sometimes can cause damage of the skin. Shaolin recipes instruct what to do in such cases.

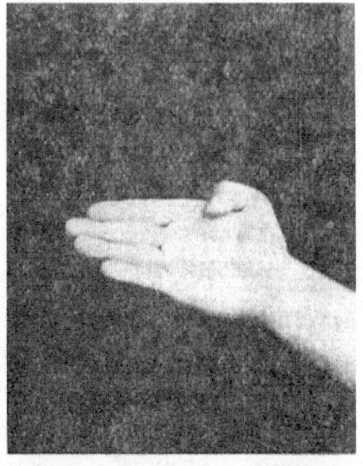

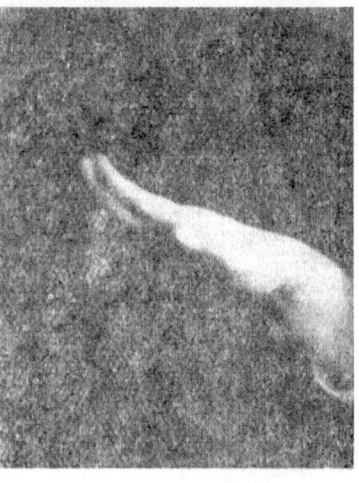

The Fifth Training Stage. Blows at Points

After finger training succeeded, one can proceed to exercise blows at points. It is a combined training which allows to fix in mind acupuncture points and channels of vital energy and find them at once. It is done in such a way: it is necessary to take a big log and made a full-scale human dummy. The dummy should have everything: head, face, arms, legs. Mark location of points with red paint. Dimensions of the marks should correspond to true dimensions (of points). Main channels should be marked with a paint of different colors.

When everything is ready, the trainee faces the dummy at a distance of one CHI (33.3 cm) approximately. Then, it is necessary to think of a point or ask somebody to name it, immediately concentrate energy at the tip of one or two fingers and touch this point. If you are sure of having done everything properly, you can proceed to a next point. It is not easy to do at the beginning, mistakes can be often made. That's why it needs everyday training, hundreds of time during a day. Gradually everything will become all right. This kind of training is conducted at a light spot in the day-time, so the sight will help fingers to get necessary spots. If you face an enemy, naturally you can employ a certain method. But is not a perfect GONG FU yet. If you wish to scale a higher level of mastery, you have to train yourself according to the above methods at night in the dark, using your sight. It is a very difficult matter, you can not get success in a short time. There is also a concealment in it. Face a wooden dummy in the dark. It is difficult for normal eyes to make out small points in darkness of the night. Even if your eyes are well-trained, all the same you see so-so. Well, how in such a case to get right to the point? There is a special technique for that. You raise your arm, estimate at which height to locate your finger tip to hit at a selected point and thrust your arm forward. The finger should be dipped into mortar before training. A white spot appears where the finger touches the wooden dummy. Have a rest after ten such white spots (ten blows) and check results. It is necessary to train yourself each day, in that case you will get success in a year.

There is one more training method – training in a lamp light (at night). You gradually decrease the brightness of the lamp until it fully extinguishes. It is a gradual method, convenient in practice, but the time needed for training extends. If you acquire this GONG FU to perfection, each blow will go home. In that case it will be no problem for you to encounter one or two enemies. Even if you are encircled by a group of enemies, you will be able of making them to lose fighting ability in a jiffy. That is nothing else but the unsurpassed skill. However, one should pay attention to applied forces that must be different depending on points which you act on. For instance, if you act on main, vital points, you must apply somewhat smaller force, because if you apply greater force, the enemy can be killed. If you do it even in self-defense, it is all the same immoral, it spoils your good deeds which will be taken into account in the world beyond. It is another matter if you act on points which are difficult to access, for example, on points deep in joints or under a thick layer of muscles. Even a coercion with a great force may not help to achieve the aim and a coercion with a small force will give no effect at all. That's why those points on a training dummy should be marked with another color to get everything in sight at once. Before acting, it is necessary to decide on the degree of force applied.

The Sixth Training Stage. Eyesight

Eyesight is a very important element in Martial Arts. Sight in any kind of WU SHU, especially in DIAN XUE, is of utmost importance. The main thing in the common WU SHU is the mobility of eyes, it is comparatively easy to attain. Besides, eyesight in DIAN XUE must be keen. One must succeed in making out small objects in darkness. It is impossible to reach such a height without hard labor. There are two training methods to acquire this skill.

The first method is as follows. Sit quietly without light each day at night. You must close your eyes, relax and imagine the location of things in your room. For instance, such and such object is in such and such place and another object is in such and such place, and so on. Or, otherwise, you can imagine a certain place in the room and fancy what things are available there. Then, open your eyes and look. At first you will see nothing. But later on, you will start to see more and more clearly. Over time you will see in darkness.

The essence of another method is as follows: use a lamp with a paper shade and gradually decrease brightness of the light until the lamp fully goes out, you have to distinguish things at that. In practice it is done so: make a shade of light-green paper and put an oil lamp inside. Over time, change the color of the paper for darker one and decrease the wick. Paper color is to be changed from light-green to black and the wick from the size of a date pit to nil. This method requires more time (compared with the first one) but it is more convenient for training from methodical point of view.

The above two methods are designed to exercise "outer" GONG FU. Although you can distinguish things in darkness, you are not able to see small details yet. It is necessary to make progress, train oneself to acquire the "inner" GONG FU. For that purpose at dawn, before sunrise, you must go to an open place, it is still better to climb a hill or mountain. Face the east and wait for the sunrise. When the sun just starts to appear on the horizon, calm down breathing, concentrate attention and look right at the sun. **[Warning: one may look at the sun only during a few minutes when the sun disk has just appeared above the line of the horizon; if you look at the risen sun fixedly, you can lose the sight!]** Some time later you will feel as if a flow of hot air goes up to the eye-sockets. At that moment you must close your eyes and move your eyeballs to the left and to the right 72 times. Make a small pause, open your eyes and look at the sun again. After it move the eyeballs again 36 times to the left and 36 times to the right. If you often do it, in a year you will see even in darkness very well. Having such eyesight plus well-trained arms, you will succeed in reaching one hundred percent hit.

The above training methods are three steps, or three stages, that make up GONG FU of the second level.

THE THIRD LEVEL OF MASTERY

The Seventh Training Stage. Impact from Distance

After reaching the second level trainees in DIAN XUE SHU are said to have acquired this kind of GONG FU to perfection. Men in command of this GONG FU, when confronting the enemy, undoubtedly have more chances to win than those who acquired common kinds of WU SHU. But its is still "outer" GONG FU. In this case fingers must still touch certain points, i.e. physical contact with the enemy is needed. If the enemy is at some distance, there will be no effect. But if you are in command of "inner" GONG FU, let the enemy be away from you even at a distance of ten steps, nevertheless, an effort like a "shot" from finger tips will reach him and stop the flow of his QI and blood. The whole body of the enemy will become rigid, he will not be able to move. Why does it happen? It is nothing else but the effect of mental effort. However, it is much more difficult to exercise mental impact than to exercise real (physical) impact.

The training method of mental impact is as follows. The first step: it is necessary to make a cup-size ball out of silk cotton and hang it on a silk thread at the place to where you often come during day-time. Each time when you come to that place make a movement with finger (or two fingers) toward the ball without touching it. Initially the ball does not move after a finger movement. Each time several finger movements should be made. Exercise it so until the ball starts swaying. It is necessary, then, to start to gradually move away from the ball up to a distance of up to eight CHIs (about 2.6 m). Then change a cotton ball with a small bag with sand. That ball is much more heavier. Go on training in the same manner and succeed in getting the same effect from a distance of eight CHIs. After that, change the bag with sand with a small bag containing little iron balls. Exercise in the same manner and succeed in swaying a bag with small iron balls weighing 12 JINs (6 kg) with a movement of one or two fingers at a distance of one ZHANG (3.33 m). It will mean that your mental effort is impressive enough. If such an effort directly affects a human body, it can make a body damage. But if the enemy wears thick clothes or armor, that effort will not give due effect and neutralize the enemy. That's why it is necessary to learn to use so-called "piercing effort". That is just "inner" GONG FU. You can not achieve success without two or three years of hard labor.

The Eighth Training Stage. Impact Through Obstacle

When we speak about a piercing impact, we mean the impact passing through an obstacle. It is not an easy matter to subdue the enemy with an usual effort. But it is twice as difficult to have an effort passed through an obstacle and hit the enemy. It could seem to profanes that these words are absurd and ridiculous. Actually one can succeed in everything with hard labor, and as the saying goes, even a steel beam can be ground off to a needle. However, exercising in this kind of GONG FU is difficult. It is done so: it is necessary to put a small oil lamp on a table and burn it; a paper screen should be put before the lamp, best of all, a screen of parchment, as it is thin and strong, which makes the passage of "impact" easier. The man stands at a distance of two CHIs (0.66 m) from the table and makes a finger movement toward the flame. During first training sessions such movement does not give visible effect on the flame because of the paper screen. But after some time the flame starts wavering as if a light wind started to blow. Then the flame wavers more and more and at last the time comes when the flame is extinguished by a movement of your hand. After it you must stay away from the table at a distance of additional two CHIs (0.66 m) and continue training until the required result is attained and so on. When, as a result of it, you step aside from the table for one ZHANG (3.33 cm), change a thin parchment for thick one. Go on training in such a way. Then change successively parchment for cardboard, glass, wooden board, and iron sheet. Strive for your "effort" to pierce through all those obstacles and extinguish the flame from a distance of one ZHANG and more. It means full success. After replacement of a screen it is necessary to increase the size of flame accordingly. When the size of flame is increased to the highest degree, change it for a candle. Then use incense, then aromatic sticks. As incense and aromatic sticks only smolder without an open flame, it is difficult to extinguish them. If you can extinguish incense through a wooden board, it means that you have reached the top. It is impossible to reach such a level of GONG FU within one or two years, it will take three, or may be even five years at least. At the end you will be able to hit the enemy even at a distance of eighteen steps and damage not only open part of his body, but "break through" his armor. If you master such GONG FU, you can withstand even a great group of enemies: you raise an arm, make a movement toward them and at once they fall down and lose the ability to resist. It is the acme of the Martial Art. But the road to it is very difficult.

The Ninth Training Stage. Practice.

At this stage you proceed to learn practical use of the knowledge you received. At previous stages you united the knowledge of points and channels with the technique of delivering blows. Now the most important thing is to avoid casual wounds, therefore it is necessary only to mark blows at points without delivering them in reality. That is the difference between a training session and a real combat. One has to strive for exactness in details and observe all key requirements for method execution.

At first, it necessary to train oneself undressed up to the waist. In that case muscles and cords are well seen on the body and owing to this it is comparatively easy to perfect particular techniques. However, it is only the first, preparatory step toward the actual acquirement of practical employment of techniques. When required exactness and knack are obtained, it is necessary to proceed to training in clothes. Over time the clothes should be changed for thicker ones and you should wear wadded and leather clothes at last. At that you must develop the ability for proper selection and use of techniques.

That is the end of the ninth training stage. At the same time that is also the end of the whole cycle aimed to acquire point striking technique. At that stage training sessions are held with a partner, therefore it is necessary to be very careful all the time, not to be rude, beware of the slightest inattentiveness in order not to damage points and channels, it is extremely important. It is necessary to clearly realize the direction of effort (blow), distinguish an "empty force" from "real force", strictly maintain wrist positions: "one finger", "two fingers", "fist like a cock's heart", "pressing palm", "sticking-into palm". In a combat one should be guided by the following principles: "Kick up a row in the east but strike in the west" and "Harass above and seize below"[30]. In that case you will seize an opportunity and win in a combat.

For instance, the point BAI HUI (1) can be pressed with a "rubbing" forward movement of a palm. The point QI MEN (12) can be impacted on with a "piercing" blow of a palm, the point TAI YANG (2) with "Two fingers like golden scissors", the point SUO XIN (?) with "Diamond finger". The point MAI WAN (19) can be impacted on with "Cock's heart", but it is necessary to fix an enemy's arm before a blow and turn its inner side to yourself, one can also seize with fingers from above and strike from below or make a grip from below and strike from above. It is possible to "cut" from the left, and "thrust" from the right. One should use different arm techniques. It is necessary to follow changes in enemy's positions and modify your actions depending on his actions. Don't stick blindly to written rules, use them according to an actual situation. In that case deadly methods that were acquired during training sessions can be used in practice with maximum effect.

Editor's notes:

[30] One of laws of military actions which implies the execution of a false dodging maneuver to strike at unprotected place.

Part III: Symptoms and Consequences of Combat Impact on Points

1. Point HUA GAI

Point HUA GAI is situated on the middle line of the torso in its upper part and belongs to the lungs channel. If a strong blow is delivered at that point, loss of consciousness occurs preceded by strong vertigo, then follows death. It is necessary to resort to medications, which help to reduce high temperature and protect the heart and the stomach against QI and blood stagnation. Primary task in it is the use of proper drugs. The consequences of a weak blow: if treatment is not timely undergone, thirteen months later unhealthy symptoms will develop it will be beyond cure.

2. Point FEI DI

If point FEI DI was hit, death will come in nine days. After a strong blow blood runs out through the nose and the death will soon follows. Medicines must be taken immediately. If not cured in good time, coughing starts in twelve months, then death follows, and no means to save life.

3. Point ZHENG QI

The point is situated on the left side, one CUN and three FENs[31] above the nipple. Called ZHENG QI[32]. Belongs to the liver channel. Twelve days after a hit at it death follows. It is

---

Editor's notes:

[31] 1 CUN is equal to 3.3 cm, 1 FEN is equal to 0.33 cm, so the mentioned distance is 4.29 cm.

[32] ZHENG QI, lit. "The true QI".

possible to avoid death only with the help of medicines. If an impact (blow) was not heavy and medications were not used, illness will develop in 48 days and death follows.

4. Point QI HAI

Point QI HAI is situated on the left side, 1 CUN and four FENs [33] below the nipple. If it is hit, death follows in 38 days. It is necessary to take medications in good time to save life.

5. Point SHANG XUE HAI

The point is situated on the right side, one CUN and three FEN[34] above the nipple. Belongs to the lungs channel. If the point is hit, death follows in 116 days. It is necessary to take medications, in that case the disease will disappear, blood flow will restore.

6. Point ZHENG XUE HAI

Point ZHENG XUE HAI is on the right side, exactly under the nipple, one CUN and three FEN below it[35]. Belongs to the lungs channel. If it is hit, hemoptysis appears and death

---

Editor's notes:

[33] Corresponds to 4.62 cm.

[34] 4.29 cm.

[35] 4.29 cm.

follows. If it is not cured in good time, death will follow in 64 days.

7. Point XIA XUE HAI

Point XIA XUE HAI is situated on the right side, under the nipple, at a distance of one CUN and four FEN from it[36]. Belongs to the lungs channel. If affected, haemorrhage and death will follow in six days. It is necessary to resort to the medicine "Thirteen tastes" immediately to save life. Without that medicine death will inevitably come.

8. Points QI XUE ER HAI

Points QI XUE ER HAI are situated on both sides of the body under the nipples, at a distance of one CUN and three FENs from them. Belong to heart, liver, and lungs. If one of those points is affected by a prick, "Three Jewels"[37] can be damaged. The three organs suffer equal damages. Death comes in seven days. It is necessary to cure with "Thirteen Tastes" urgently. If the medicine is not properly taken, certain death will come in 56 days.

Editor's notes:

[36] 4.62 cm.

[37] That is the three above-mentioned organs.

9. Point HEI HU

Point HEI HU is situated in the region of the solar plexus. If it is affected, vertigo and a sense of drunkenness appear. Treatment with the medicine "Thirteen tastes" is urgently needed. If medicines are not taken, death will follow in 100 days. If the point is severely attacked (to deliver a strong blow) with a fist in the shape of "cock's heart", death follows immediately, life can not be saved. An attack with fingers in a pinch causes death in twenty days, treatment will not save life.

10. Point HUO FEI

Point HUO FEI is situated one CUN and three FENs[38] below the solar plexus. Belongs to the heart channel. If it is hit, it immediately goes dark before one's eyes and one has appearance of being drunk. If a place half-FEN[39] below point FEI DI is pressed and then rubbed with the edge of a palm, you "sober up" immediately. The point is also called HUI GUI – "The Point that brings back the demon". When wounded, it is necessary to take medicines. If it is left without treatment, a fatal illness appears in 120 days, then life can not be saved.

―――――――――――――――

Editor's notes:

[38] 4.29 cm.

[39] About 1.6 mm.

11. Point FAN DU

Point FAN DU is situated on the left of the solar plexus at a distance of one CUN and three FEN[40]. Belongs to the liver channel. If it is strongly hit, one can die at the same day. If the disease is not cured, death can follow in 120 days and no treatment will save.

12. Point FU QI

Point FU QI belongs to two channels: the small intestine channel and the spleen channel. After it is hit, death follows in 28 days. It is necessary to use medicines. If they are not used, an illness occurs in one month and death follows, treatment becomes impossible.

13. Point DIEN TIAN

Point DIEN TIAN is situated one CUN and three FENs[41] below the navel. It has two more names – FEN SHUI and JIN HAI. Belongs to the small intestine and kidneys channels. If it is severely hit, death follows in nine days. If a blow is not so heavy but it is not treated with medicines, death follows after 49 days, it will be beyond cure.

Editor's notes:

[40] 4.29 cm.

[41] 4.29 cm.

14. Point ZHENG FEN SHUI

Point ZHENG FEN SHUI is situated at a distance of one CUN and four FENs[42] below the navel. Belongs to the bladder channel. That place is a point to which QI of the small intestine and the large intestine flows. If the point is hit, constipation in the small and large intestines occurs and in fourteen days follows death. The medicine "Thirteen tastes" must be taken immediately. If symptoms are not cured completely, death will follow in 184 days, it will be beyond cure.

15. Point QI GE

Point QI GE is situated two CUNs[43] below the navel, on the left side of the peritoneum. If it is hit, death will follow in 180 days. If symptoms are not treated in time and to the end, death will follow in one year.

16. Point GUAN YUAN

Point GUAN YUAN is situated one CUN and three FENs[44] below the navel and five FENs15 to the right. If the point is hit, death follows in five days. Urgent treatment with the medicine "Thirteen tastes" is needed. In case of improper

---

Editor's notes:
[42] 4.62 cm.
[43] 6.6 cm.
[44] 4.29 cm.

treatment, without uprooting the illness, swelling appears in 24 days and it inevitably leads to death, treatment will be impossible.

17. Point XUE HAI MEN

The point is situated on the right side, two CUNs[45] below the navel. After an impact on this point a man can perish in 147 days.

18. Point QI MEN

The point is situated on the left side where the cartilage and muscles are connected together. After an impact on this point the man can perish in 120 days. If the cure is not completed, he can perish in 240 days.

19. Point XUE NANG

The point is situated on the right side, two FENs[46] below the cartilage. After an impact on this point the man can perish in 42 days. If the cure is not completed, he will perish in twelve months.

Editor's notes:

[45] 6.6 cm.
[46] 0.66 cm.

20. Point XUE CANG QI MEN

The point is situated on the right side, eight FENs[47] below ribs where soft tissue is available. After an impact on this point the man will perish in 60 days. With improper treatment he will die in one year.

21. Point QI XUE NANG HE

The point is under the left armpit, one FEN[48] below it. QI and blood (XUE) meet at that place, that is why it is called QI XUE NANG HE. After an impact on this point the man will perish in 42 days. If the cure is not completed, he will live not more than three months.

22. Point DU MAI

The point is situated on the bone of the back of the head, at the junction of the three main channels. If this bone is crushed, a man dies on the spot, if a blow is not so heavy, in 5-7 days. If the cure is not completed, there will be a regular pain in the region of the back of the head and it will spread over the whole body.

Editor's notes:

[47] 2.64 cm.
[48] 0.33 cm.

23. Point ZHEN E

The center of the forehead belongs to the heart channel. After an impact there is no open wound, but the head will be stupefied. The man will perish in six or seven days.

24. Point DA CHANG MING MEN

Points TAI YANG TAI YING and DA CHANG MING MEN are situated on the sides of the head. After a heavy impact (a blow) the man will perish in seven days and after a lighter impact (a blow), in fifteen days. There may appear symptoms of ears and eyes affection, internal bruises, suppuration; however, the man can be alive. But if symptoms similar to the symptoms of catching cold and a swelling appear, the lethal outcome is quite probable. If not treated, nine out of ten men perish.

25. Point JIANG XUE

These points are situated at the top of ears. They are called JIANG XUE and SHAO YIN JING and belong to the kidneys channel and JIU E YIN channel. If they are heavily hit, the man perishes from asphyxia on the spot. A lighter impact leads to a swelling and the man will perish within forty days. If the cure is not completed, the man will perish in 56 days.

26. Point YIN TANG MEI XIN

The point is situated on the bridge of the nose, one CUN[49] below frontal bone. After a blow at this point a swelling appears and a man perishes within three days. An open wound that bleeds is not dangerous. A hidden trauma and a swelling are beyond cure, the man perishes.

27. Points XUE RU, ZHUO MIN, CHO NAN MIN, HEI HU XIN, GUI YIN, YOU HUN XUE

After a heavy impact on any of these six points the man perishes. But if the impact is not heavy, he can be cured. If bones are crushed, nine out of ten men perish unless some family secret recipe is not used.

28. Points SHEN MING XUE

All points and channels on the back are connected to the kidneys. Among them points SHEN MING XUE are "deadly". They are situated on both sides of the seventh vertebra, one FEN below it, where soft tissue is available. After a heavy impact coughing with phlegm and blood appears, the man perishes within one year. If the cure is not completed, the man perishes in fourteen months.

Editor's notes:

[49] 3.3 cm.

29. Points HOU HAI

The points are a bit outward from SHEN MING XUE and one CUN and eight FENs[50] below them. After an impact on them the man will perish in 33 days or in 64 days if the cure is not completed.

30. Points YAO YAN

They are situated under points HOU HAI on the waist at a distance of one CUN and three FENs[51]. The left point is connected to the kidneys and the right one is "deadly". After an impact on it the man starts laughing and perishes in three days. It is incurable without medicines.

31. Point MING MEN

The point is situated on the right of the kidney. If it is hit, the man will be in coma and perish in a day.

Editor's notes:

[50] 5.94 cm.

[51] 4.29 cm

32. Point CHOU HAI DI

The point is situated two FENs[52] below the coccyx. After an impact on it the man will perish in seven days. If the cure is not completed, the man perishes from jaundice in one year.

33. Point HE KOU

These points are situated on feet. If they are severely hit, the man will perish in one year. If the cure is not completed, the man will become an incurable insane.

34 Point YONG QUAN

The point is situated on the sole of a foot. After a heavy impact on it the man will perish in fourteen months. However, early medical aid can save the man.

Editor's notes:
[52] 0.66 cm.

Above are mentioned 34 points. After a heavy impact on them the man perishes at once and after a relatively weak impact he can be saved. In case of a "weak" impact the man does not feel pain and symptoms of the impact may not be revealed immediately, therefore it needs early treatment. If the treatment is of small efficiency, it means that a serious internal damage was inflicted on the man. The treatment of affected points and channels mainly consists of taking medicines, but one must be careful and cautious at that.

Points That Save From Death

Those who learn military skills must be able not only to do harm but also be able to give a help for a man. It is necessary to be able not only to kill but to save as well. Otherwise your skill will be one-sided, because only "deadly" techniques acquired is the common WU SHU. If you strictly observe this rule, your acquirement of DIAN XUE SHU will be deepest.

The common WU SHU is characterized with methods which inflict wounds, it is its main aim, there is no need to trouble about somebody's life. If you are unable to cure yourself, instead of using DIAN XUE SHU you can see a doctor who specializes in traumatology. But a specialist who treats traumas and who received his knowledge from previous generations must know point impact techniques and laws of their use. Lack of knowledge of those laws can be of great harm, because if you have no drugs at hand, only point impact methods can be of help. Therefore, if you know point locations, you can cure yourself.

Basic principles of DIAN XUE SHU are rather simple. If QI and blood flow slows down at some place and sometime even stops, it becomes apparent in general constraint of the whole body. If there is a chance to open these "doors", it means that there is a chance to restore normal QI and blood flow. In that case the channels JIN and MAI restore their activity and diseases disappear all by itself. If some point is "closed" for some time, QI and blood will be stuck and accumulate at that point. The method of treatment in that case will be preparation of this point for unhampered passage of body substances through it.

At that, it is also necessary "to open" neighboring points along that meridian. "Closed" points can be dangerous centers of pathology inside the body. It is, therefore, necessary to gradually restore normal QI and blood flow at that point. If the point is "closed" long time ago, QI and blood in that region have a tendency to clotting, even stagnation, haemostasia, bruise, et cetera can occur. Therefore, it is necessary to take treatment and drugs and cure concomitant diseases with them. Otherwise, suppuration will get into the organism, which would obstruct free movement of QI and blood, new centers of stagnation can appear, and body substances can not freely circulate. It will lead to hard consequences, in the worst case one can become an invalid. It should be treated very seriously.

Part IV: Training Methods for Fingers Hardening

(From the book by Jin Jing Zhong "Training Methods of 72 Arts of Shaolin", Tanjin, 1934)

Method "Diamond Finger"(YI ZHI JIN GANG FA)

The method "Diamond Finger" is a "hard" exercise that strengthens the external components[53]. It belongs to the "hard" force of YANG. When the exercise attains its aim, it is possible to knock a hole in the chest with a finger and injure internal organs. When mastering this exercise, one should train his finger daily on a wall or a tree trunk, other objects can be also used. It is necessary to 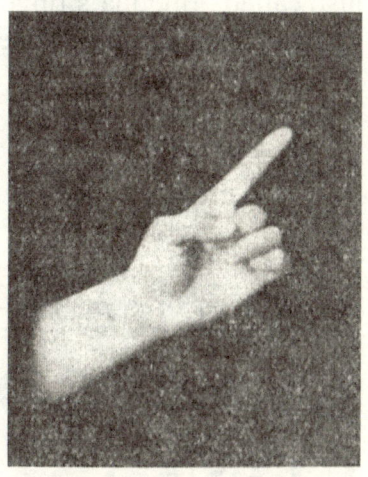 strike with your forefinger at a wall or other objects, starting with a slight blow and increasing gradually its force. Don't interrupt and don't stop your training. It is the first stage on the path to mastership. The skin tears off, muscles and sinews swell and hurt, but it is necessary to continue training for a long time without any hesitation and doubts. The soft skin

Editor's notes:

[53] **Strengthening of such external parameters as skin, muscles and bones is meant.**

becomes hard. After three years of training the finger will become like a tree brunch. If you strike at some object with your finger, a visible finger print is left on it. A blow at a wood can make a hollow in it, a blow at a stone can break it, a blow at a humane body can inflict a serious wound. Train this exercise diligently for three years, concentrate efforts only on one matter and your skill will become perfect if you have inflexible will. Indeed, there are outstanding men who make every effort. Beware of mistakes and wounds and move to the planned aim. One can also train the forefinger of the left hand. Don't stop at the midway in this exercise! This GONG FU is also called "Buddha's finger". There are even verses that can be read when doing this exercise. But regularity in training is a must.

Exercise "Pulling out Nails" (BO DING GONG)

The exercise "Pulling out Nails" belongs to hard external training, it is the hard YANG force. It is one of the exercises which develop skill of hands, the locking force of thumb, forefinger and middle finger. The exercise is very simple. It is necessary to take a thick unabi, or jujube board[54], knock 108

Editor's notes:
[54] Unabi, Jujube - a small tree, bearing date-like fruit and growing in China.

nails with length of about 3 CUNs (10 cm) into it and pull them out with the thumb and forefinger.

If you can pull out nails with your hand, that is the end of the first stage on the way to mastership.

Then, drive nails into a wooden board, sprinkle them with water, wait when the nails become rusty and pull them out as it was described above. If you are able to pull out nails with your hand, your skill has reached the highest point. It is a difficult exercise at the first stage, the skin bursts, blisters bleed, that's why it is necessary to wash hands with warm solution of lake salt[55] with other ingredients after you finish doing the exercise. One may pull out 1000 nails at the last stage. In a fight you can make locks with three fingers for vulnerable spots (according to acupoints and channels) and heavily injure your enemy.

Editor's notes:

[55] "The salt from the lake of QING HAI" in the Chinese original.

Exercise "One Finger of Chan Meditation" (YI ZHI CHAN GONG)

YI ZHI CHAN in 72 Shaolin Martial Arts belongs to the category YIN. It is one of the most deadly methods among the soft kinds of GONG FU. The gist of mastership is in one finger. Xi Hei Zi, a well-known master of the Southern Shaolin school, is in full command of this kind of GONG FU. He studied the Martial Arts during 40 years, visited all southern and northern provinces and no man was able to overcome him.

At the very beginning when he started training, he hung a weight at the place where he often passed along at day-time. Each time, when he passed it, he poked his finger to it. He did it each time from day to day. At the beginning, when he poked his finger to the weight, it remained motionless. Then, being struck, it started to swing. After it he increased the distance between him and the weight and his finger did not touch the weight when hitting. He struck at emptiness in the direction of the weight and it started to swing. If you reach this point, you may think that you have done the first step on the way to mastering YI ZHI CHAN.

Then he put a few lamps in the court and lighted them at night. He stood before the lamps at a distance of two

ZHANG[56] and delivered a blow with one finger. At first the flame of a lamp only swayed like it sways from a light wind. However, after some time one finger striking toward the lamp immediately extinguished the flame. It is the second stage in mastering this kind of GONG FU. After it, it is necessary to put paper shades on lamps and train oneself until striking with one finger tears paper and extinguishes flame. That is the end of the third stage. And, at last, paper shades are replaced with glass ones. When striking with one finger flame extinguishes and the glass does not get broken, it means that the aim has been attained. It needs 10 years of tenacious work. If this mastership is directed against a man, there will be no wounds seen, but the internal organs will be seriously injured. A weak blow in direction of some aqupoints can cause vascular spasm and block blood circulation. After it blood circulation can be restored only with special massage. This GONG FU is much more serious than "The Palm of Red Shot", "The Palm of Black Shot" and "Hands of Five Poisons". The only thing you need is regularity, and success will come.

Editor's notes:

[56] ZHANG is measure of length equal to 3.33 m.

Skill "Piercing Through Stones" (DIEN SHI GONG)

It is possible to obtain a result only by making tremendous efforts and spending much time.

The skill "Piercing Through Stones" serves for strengthening the "outer" power of the body, it is designed to rear the YANG force in a human body. That skill is aimed at training the "indicative force" of two fingers. After mastering it you can kill a man, just touching him with your hand. As regard to its effectiveness, it is similar to some "soft" exercises for finger training.

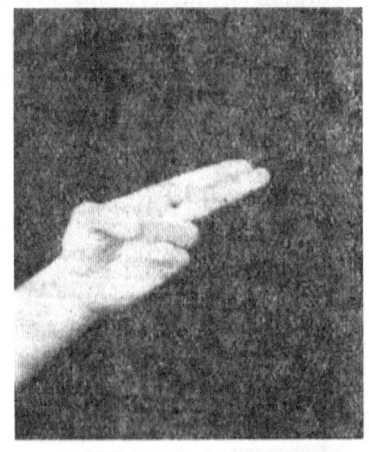

When you master the skill DIEN SHI GONG, you will be able to concentrate all your force in fingers, or in finger tips, to speak more correctly. Using only fingers, it is possible to do a lot of harm to the health of a man, moreover, it is possible to inflict severe wounds in him. You will be able to hit a man, even if some physical obstacle separates you from him. At that, it is necessary to indicate directly at the man whose health you would like to do harm. Only in that case the use of that skill will have the highest efficiency. It should be realized well and kept in mind from the start of training.

When you finish learning the exercise, you will be able to hit easily people only with your fingers and inflict on them severe wounds, even those ones that cause death. If one needs to cure such wounds with herbal medicine, he has to cure the whole body. If only fingers are capable of inflicting such body damages, what could you say about the whole arm and the destructive force which can be contained in it?

The method to acquire the skill is a simplest one. It is necessary to press two fingers (forefinger and middle finger) to each other and stretch them forward. The fourth finger and the little finger should be bent so that their pads may touch the center of the palm and be pressed strongly to it. The thumb should be pressed to the fourth finger and the little finger from above. Thus, the hand should look like that one squeezing the sword JIAN. Then, point finger tips that are stretched forward at some object and as if prick it with strength. That skill should be developed during many days.

It is best of all to train oneself in the beginning as follows: take some amount of soft soil, carefully pound it, mix it with liquid glue until it becomes stringy, wrap in a piece of cloth and leave it to dry up (to harden). Than draw a great number of small circles (on the cloth) with a middle-sized brush for writing hieroglyphs. Later, it will be necessary to thrust your fingers, fold as above, into the circles. At first, it is necessary to use one circle and prick it with fingers until a recess appears in it. Later, it will be necessary to make a recess in the second circle etc.

It is necessary to increase gradually number of exercises with each recess to make them ever deeper. So, daily number of exercises with each hole must reach ten. After two years of such training when you can easily pierce through the earth you may proceed to exercises with light stones. The principle of doing the exercises will remain the same as that one with earth.

Two more years later, when you can easily pierce through stones, the skill DIEN SHI GONG will have been mastered. At present this skill in use is as effective as in the past. Having acquired the technique, you yourself will have to understand the importance of this exercise for the Martial Art. Don't be blind, try to understand clearly the meaning of learning DIEN SHI GONG. The man who learns and improves the method must be very persistent from the very beginning. Training one of the skills of "Deadly Hand", he must concentrate his utmost attention to it without stopping to learn in no time. It is not so easy just to stretch an arm and inflict on a man such injuries that will cause death. Trainees who pay attention to all those things will master the skill "Piercing Through Stones" to perfection.

After it one may proceed to learn the skill of striking at vulnerable points DIAN XUE SHU to become more powerful.

Rubbing Palms (HE PAN ZHANG)

If somebody practices in squeezing various things with force, it is a good method to learn to twist even the hardest things. Later, even an iron chopstick can be knotted and pressed so that it will become very thin and its length will increase as much as twice. It is only doubtful if that chopstick will be still suitable for application.

The technique "Rubbing[57] Palms", sometimes called "Hand of Golden Dragon", is the most effective among all known methods of the pugilistic art which are anyhow connected to "rubbing" movements. Training in this technique is also aimed at strengthening outer power of the body and rearing the YANG force in it.

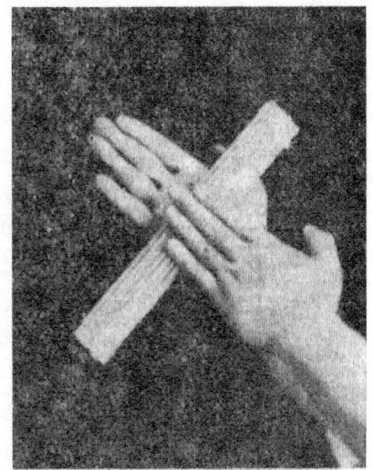

The method of acquiring the technique "Rubbing Palms" is very and very simple. Take 30 bamboo chopsticks, best of all, square ones. Gather the sticks

---

Editor's notes:

[57]"Twisting", "wrenching", "pressing" etc. in this text imply the same movement, that is: palms are put together (as in a prayer) with a thing (a bunch of chopsticks) pressed between them, palms move back and forth in respect to each other, it is the movement when one rubs palms.

in one bundle and tie it up with a thin thread in several places. It is necessary to tie the sticks so that not to leave even a millimeter of space between them. The sticks must be pressed to each other so tightly that they may not move. Surely, it will be difficult for you at first to tie chopsticks so. If there is space left between them, keep inserting more sticks there until your bunch has the proper view.

Then you have to take the chopsticks with both hands, press them between the palms and rub the bunch to roll on each of your palms. It should be done with force. The left palm must also move in respect to the right one and turn the bunch with force. When you are exhausted, take a little rest. Then squeeze the bunch of sticks again in your palms and rub it with all your strength between the palms. This exercise should be done several times each day.

Over time chopsticks will be pressed in a bunch ever tighter. At last, they will be so close to each other, that even a silk thread can not be thrust through them. After two years when you make a little progress in learning HE PAN ZHANG, the outer sticks if twisted will start to break and intertwine and the inner sticks to turn over, though the bunch is tightly fixed with threads. Now you may proceed to training with metal chopsticks.

The training method with metal chopsticks does not differ from that one with bamboo sticks. After two years when metal thumb-thick sticks are thinned to a thickness of small fingers and the length of the sticks increases as much as twice or more, it will mean that you have made every effort "during 1000 days" and it will be seen by naked eye. At that moment it will become clear that you have fully mastered the skill. It is beyond any doubts now that you will be able to cope with any thing just by stretching an arm and touching it. You will be able to break something instantly, crumple any iron or stone thing. Nothing can resist you strongly, not to mention men of flesh and blood.

A great wizard from Jiangnan, the inventor of this exercise, described it in his book. He related that when somebody acquires this method, wood will seem to him as soft as vegetables. You will be able to break a bamboo into small pieces, fray a steel rope with your fingers. The only thing you need to do is to stretch your arm and touch a gate, and the most strongest bolts will be opened. There is still a vast number of methods of application of that skill. Surely, that technique can be effectively used for repelling an enemy's attack.

They say even a steel pole can be ground off into a needle with a profound mastery in stock.

Cinnabar Palm (ZHU SHA ZHANG)

"Cinnabar Palm" is the soft GONG FU, it trains the inner power and belongs to category YIN. This exercise is also called "The Palm of Plum Blossom" (MEI HUA ZHANG) and "Palm of Red Sand" (HONG SHA ZHANG). Sometimes it is also called "Hand of Black Sand", but that is not right, because the method of "Hand of Black Sand" involves the use of special preparations to increase the inner power.

Training method: fill a tub with fine sand, immerse your hands into sand and rub them with force until you exhaust. It should be done each day in order to finally reach such level of mastership that when rubbing your hands over the tub at a distance of one CHI (30 cm) sand in it will move in unison with hands. It means that the first stage in mastering this kind of GONG FU is over. If you

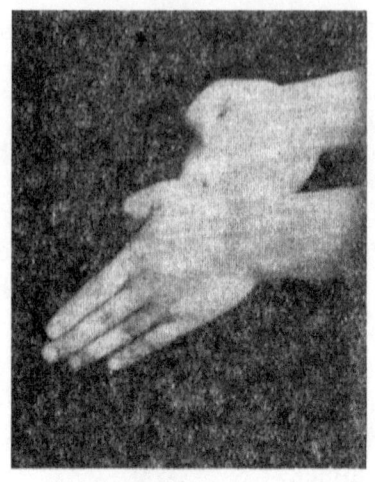

strike a man after that, only slightly touching his body, no outer injuries will be seen, but the inner organs will be severely, incurably wounded. While continue training, it is necessary to replace fine sand with iron shot, which later on should be replaced with iron balls weighing 4-5 LIANs[58]. If your hands do not touch the tub and the iron balls start moving after your hands, it means that the art of "Cinnabar Palm" has been mastered. If you are in command of this GONG FU, you need not touch the enemy with hands. You make stroking movements or strike with a palm at some distance and the enemy is severely injured and will surely die in 10-15 days or even in several hours. But at least 15 years of hard work are needed to attain such skill. Being in command of this GONG FU, you must not misuse it in any case. It is a manifestation of guile and ill intentions to use it secretly. It can be used only in extremity to defend your life or the life of your near relatives. Unfounded use of this skill is immoral and disapproved by specialists in WU SHU.

Editor's notes:

[58] 1 LIAN is equal to 1/16 JIN, or 31 grams.

Technique of "Rubbing and Thrusts" (MO CHA SHU)

The technique of "Rubbing and Thrusts" belongs to "hard" and "external" exercises, it is "hard" Yang force as to its character, but at the same time it also strengthens the inner spirit. The training method is rather simple and understandable, that skill is used in such techniques as "Methods of impact on acupoints" (DIAN XUE SHU), "Methods of impact on bones" (YU GU FA) and other basic methods of Gong Fu.

The method of training is as follows. Stand up and put feet together at the first gleam of light in the East. It is necessary to stand freely, close the mouth and "hide the tongue"[59], reach complete composure. After jointing both palms, rub them 20 times on each other. At first, lay the right palm on the center of your chest, and the left palm on your spine. Thus, both palms face each other. Do 40-50 rubbings with palms, making circular movements. Then, move the right palm to the back and the left palm to the center of the chest and do 40-50 rubbings as above described. You must not breathe out through the mouth, use the nose for breathing, imagine how the breast is filled with QI.

Editor's notes:

[59]"Hide the tongue" means that the mouth is closed, the tongue is behind teeth and touches the upper palate.

After some quite long time you will feel the single refined QI roll into a ball, QI concentrates in the chest like a pulsating pearl ball. Wait until the ball increases and fill the whole chest. In that case the refined QI reaches the surface of the breast and begins to inspissate. From here QI moves very slowly to both hands and from the hands reaches finger tips.

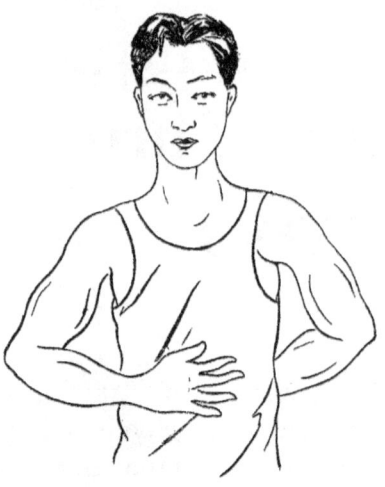

Then, take a box filled with beans and make thrusts with fingers. Both hands move in turn, one hand raises, the second one lowers, number of repeated movements in the exercise depends upon physical ability of a trainee. It is necessary to do the exercise until painful feeling appears. One should keep in mind the number of thrusts and gradually, day after day, increase them. For example, do 100 times during the

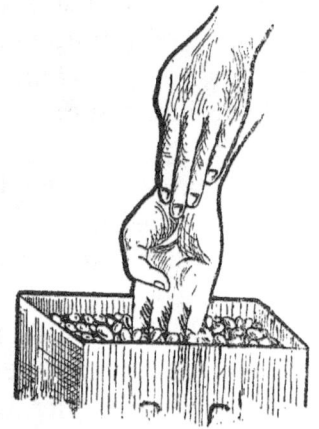

first day, 105 times during the second day and increase the duration of this exercise gradually to the time needed for burning off an aromatic stick[60]. That is the first stage in obtaining mastery. After that, beans should be replaced with

---

Editor's notes:

[60] Apparently about 40 minutes, although the original text does not give any indications as to the size of an aromatic stick.

rice grains, continue to do the exercise as before and increase the duration of the exercise to the time needed for burning off an aromatic stick. That is the end of the second stage. Now a box with rice should be replaced with a box with sand, continue to train yourself according to the same pattern and use the time of burning off an aromatic stick as a guidance. At that stage you will reach full success in mastering the skill MO CHA SHU.

As mentioned before, the exercise should be done before getting into bed and at dawn. After its acquirement it is necessary to learn the technique of point impact DIAN XUE SHU, and after it you will be able to use your mastery in practice more effectively. After practising the exercise during one year it will be possible to learn the technique of point impact, and it will be the second level of mastery. Training and strengthening fingers is a base, it is impossible to reach full success in learning the point technique DIAN XUE SHU without it.

A wooden box for that exercise should be made of unabi tree or elm, its area should be two square CHIs (about 50 x 50 cm), its height may be about one CHI (33 cm). The box is filled with soybeans, then  common rice, then yellow sand (or yellow clay). When you acquire steady skills, you can proceed to iron filings and gradually increase the duration of training session to the time needed for burning off an aromatic stick. After that your fingers will become as hard as iron and you will be able to make a hole in a chest or tear stomach muscles. It is strictly obligatory to wash your hands with heated medical solution after finishing the exercise with iron filings to eliminate swelling and damages in such a way, it is necessary to pay a great deal of attention to it.

Exercise "Jumping Centipede" (WU GONG TIAO)

The exercise "Jumping Centipede" is also called "The Art of Slithering Snake" (SHE XING SHU). It trains arm and leg skills well and spring ability at the same time.

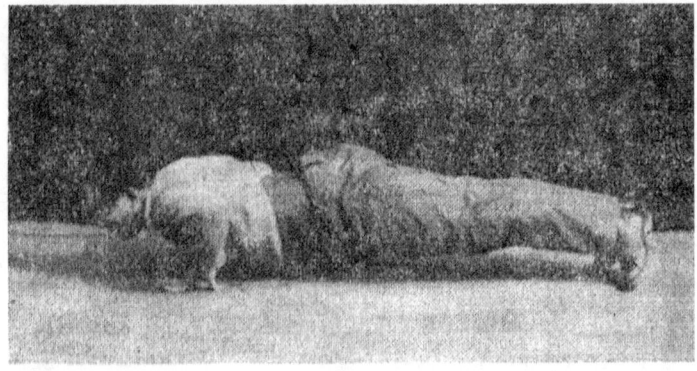

Training method: both hands with the palms and both feet with the toes take a firm stand on the ground, holding the whole body suspended. The breast and the stomach are at a distance of 6-9 cm from the ground level. This is the starting position for the exercise. Then the lower part of the body rises a little up due to bending in the waist, at the same time both palms push off the ground with force, the toes of both feet also push off (the ground), the pushing force being directed upward and a little backward. The whole body flies up and "hangs over" in the air. Using the force of a push, it is necessary not only to jump up, but also move forward, then land to the palms and the toes and take a firm stand on the ground; as before, the torso is at a distance of 6-9 cm from the ground level. In such a way, the initial position is assumed.

When a certain level of skill is attained in this exercise, the palms may be clenched into fists, then proceed to a support on five fingers, three fingers, two fingers and, finally, one finger (forefinger). One may also raise one foot and continue doing the exercise until it is possible to make jumps in any direction – either forward or backward. The exercise is considered to be worked through at this stage. If you encounter the enemy, the force of fingers and toes will help to overwhelm him; moreover, jumps can be used for retreat in a fight. You can press yourself close to the ground and slither like a snake if the enemy suddenly rushed to you and you could not foresee this.

Celestial's Palm (XIAN REN ZHANG)

The exercise "Celestial's Palm" belongs to hard exercises for outer strengthening. This exercise trains to obtain so called "YANG Hand", it trains the skill of stabbing force of finger tips. There is a similar, on the face of it, exercise for a hand YIN, the soft exercise "One Finger of CHAN Meditation" (YI ZHI CHAN GONG). However, those two exercises are similar only in that in both cases finger tips are used. Four fingers closely laid together are used in this exercise. The training method is quite simple and one can achieve a good result comparatively soon, therefore many people do it.

The method of doing the exercise: at first press together four fingers tightly, (the fingers are straight and strained) and deliver stabbing blows with force at hard objects, for instance at wall, tree, table or wooden bench. At the first stage it is not essential that it should be a definite object. Training must be carried out each day. After long training some result will be achieved, for instance, 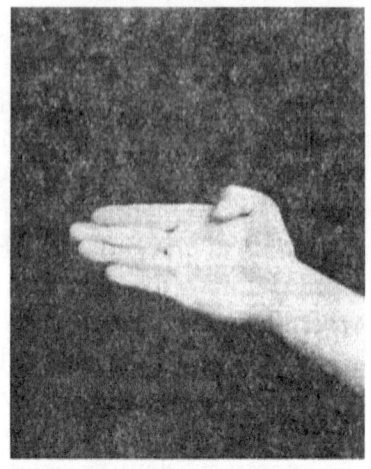 you will be able to make a small dent in a wood. The more you train, the more will be the dent, with time you will strike a hole. Take then a big stone - a green semiprecious stone - and continue training as before. With time, after many blows, you will make a deep dent. If you deliver a blow at an enemy with this palm, you will inflict on him a severe wound. Therefore, one should be quiet and well-balanced. Even those who improve their skill in "Iron Bull" (TIE NIU GONG)[61] and bear sword and spear blows with confidence, will not be able withstand. It is of no importance whether he knows about this technique or not: when he comes across with "Celestial's Palm", he will surely lose. A trainee in "Iron Bull" exercises hard force of YANG. Although a trainee in "Celestial's Palm" also exercises the hard force of YANG, but the soft force of

---

Editor's notes:

[61] See for detail: Jin Jing Zhong. Training Methods of 72 Arts of Shaolin. Tanjin, 1934. You can order this book here: www.kungfulibrary.com.

YIN is also available, therefore YIN overpowers YANG. It is called "to overpower hardness with the help of softness". There is such a saying among fighters: "Training the exercise "Iron Bull", it is possible to attain perfection, but this skill becomes ineffectual against "Celestial's Palm".

When training this skill, it is better to exercise both left and right palm, in that case the enemy will not know from where a blow will be delivered. Two words (hieroglyphs) JIAN and REN – "Tenacity" and "Endurance" can be the best wishes.

Exercise "Finger Lock" (SUO ZHI GONG)

It is a soft exercise that strengthens inside, it belongs to the soft force of YIN, but also develops the hard force of YANG at the same time. This specialized exercise for strengthening finger tips has great similarity to and some difference with such methods as "Force of Eagle Claws" (YING ZHAO LI) and "Making Holes in Stones" (DIAN SHI GONG)[62]. All those exercises form so called "Deadly Arm" (SHA SHOU)[63].

Editor's notes:

[62] See for detail: Jin Jing Zhong. Training Methods of 72 Arts of Shaolin. Tanjin, 1934. You can order this book here: www.kungfulibrary.com.

[63] Hieroglyph SHA has a meaning "to kill", "deadly", "lethal" and also "hard", "rigid", "stiff".

Differences between them are given below. For instance, the exercise "Force of Eagle Claws" trains the force of fingers for locks and the exercise "Making Holes in Stones" trains the ability to deliver thrusts with finger tips. "Finger Lock" also trains finger tips for seizing movements but differs from two previous skills in training methods and methods of use.

Training method: at the first stage of mastering this skill, squeeze together two fingers – the middle finger and forefinger tightly and join them after bending to the bent thumb. All three fingers tightly join each other with their tips. A hollow is formed in the center of the palm, the spot between the thumb and the forefinger (HU KOU, literally "tiger's mouth") makes a circle. Press your fingers with 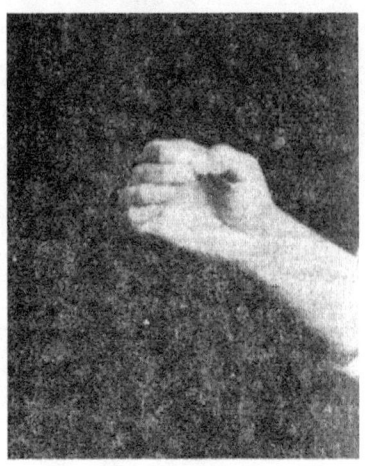 force like a cook taking seasoning. Keep them a little in this position, then open and have a rest. Then, press tightly again with force. Do the exercise each day in your spare time without limiting number of repetitions. When pressing fingers, it is necessary to use the force of the whole arm, send it to the tips of three fingers, concentrate the Spirit and collect QI.

After one year of pertinacious training the lock will become strong. At that time, take a piece of board, 3 or 4 cm thick, squeeze it between fingers, continue to train you as before and try to press a hole through the board with fingers. It is the first step on the way to mastership and it may take more than two years, but it can take less than one year with diligence. Then, continue to train you as before with an iron plate. It is necessary to seek for the plate to be dented with fingers.

Mastership reaches perfection at that stage. Four to five years of persistent training may pass from the start of familiarization with the exercise to its completion. If after successful mastering this GONG FU, you seize some part of the enemy's body with three fingers, you will surely crush his muscles or splinter his bones, inflicting a very severe wound on him.

Exercise "PIPA" (PIPA GONG)

The exercise "PIPA" is also called SAN YIN ZHI – "Three Fingers of Yin" and ZHI TOU TAN - "Springy Fingers". This exercise is specialized on strengthening the outer side of finger tips and nails. It is a "hard" exercise belonging to the YANG force, a special exercise for the development of the "flicking" force of fingers. When training fingers (in other exercises), one finger, either the forefinger or the middle finger, is often used. In the exercise "PIPA" four fingers which do springy movements (flicks) in turn are used. It resembles playing PIPA, the Chinese guitar: as if fingers run over strings, hence that name of the exercise. It is necessary to do flicks with finger nails with force; however, one should try to do those operations softly enough and as a result you will master the "soft" part of the exercise. When you succeed in training this ("soft") part, it will be enough for keeping the enemy in check efficiently. They say, it seems to be simple, but only that who really seeks to reach mastership and shows endurance for a long time will get a good result. It is unlike other kinds of "hard" skills in which it is as easy as pie to get good results.

However, one can not help but resort to medicines, one has to eliminate shortcomings by some auxiliary means too. Follow the given recipe for training, select required components and use it externally: mix white vinegar and white salt, 5 kg each component, put them into a caldron and heat for one hour. Then, remove sediments from the mixture, add 5 kg of sand from a lake, put that into a stone 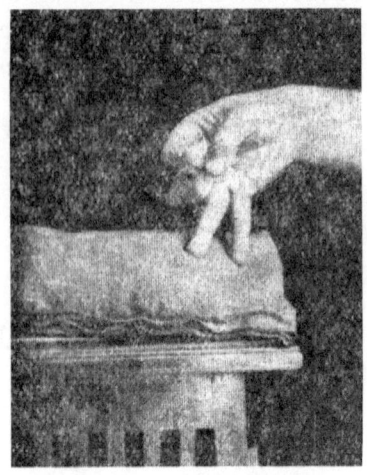 mortar and pound into small particles, fill a bag of thick fabric with obtained powder. Put the bag on a strong wooden bench, smooth the bag out and wait until it becomes dry and hard, turning into one piece. After that it can be used.

Training method: lay tightly all five fingers in the region of nails and do springy flicks with four fingers in turn with force. Start from the forefinger, then the middle finger, the ring finger, the little finger follow, again the little finger, the ring finger, the middle finger and the forefinger. Continue to do the exercise in such a manner. Hit the bag 108 times each day, in the morning and in the evening. After three-year training you will be able to get results. If you deliver a blow at the enemy by means of a "flick", the effect will be different from that one of "Diamond Finger" or other techniques with which the chest or the stomach can be pierced, but it will be enough to subdue the enemy. At the same time this technique can be employed so that it will lead to inevitable death (of the enemy) and no medicine can save him. After hitting the enemy no traces are seen outside, but a severe injury is inflicted inside. This method as well as the exercise "Finger like Spring" and all other kinds of YIN hand methods belong to so called methods of "Wolfish Poison" (LANG DU)[64], therefore there is a ban on transfer of this knack to ordinary people among fighters. That one who trains this skill has outer distinctive peculiarities: the nails of his four fingers that did the exercise are of black color, and owing to that nail blackness he differs from ordinary (people). At the same time (the color of) his thumb nail that is not used in the exercise is like that one of an ordinary man. Poor QI and blood circulation after training for a long time according that method accounts for that, this phenomenon appears on the people who practice this method. When you meet an enemy, you can know his technique from the above indications and be on guard. If you don't master the skill of the "YIN Hand", you should politely bow and leave, otherwise you can be seriously wounded.

Although this skill belongs to "hard" force of Yang, the exact tool of QI is softness Yin, and if those two principles are linked, the skill will be superb. One must not bring the situation to a threat of life or injuries, one must not abuse this skill. Otherwise, by striking ("flicking") with two fingers, a man can be wounded so that he will not be able to restore his health. There is the demand for modesty in the "Secret Virtue"[65] YIN DE and a combatant, training that difficult exercise, must always keep it in mind.

Editor's notes:

[64] LANG DU has an additional meaning – "cruelty", "treachery".

[65] YIN DE has an additional meaning – feminine, passive element of the nature, female virtue.

Exercise "Pinching a Flower" (NIAN HUA GONG)

It is a very refined exercise, but (it is necessary to keep) constancy! After successful acquirement (of the exercise) you can not only kill people, but effect on acupoints with your fingers like needles used in zhen jiu[66] and save human life.

The exercise "Pinching a flower" belongs to "soft" exercises for "external" strengthening. It is the YIN "soft" force as to its kind. It is one of exercises which specialize in strengthening finger tips, small parts in human extremities. Their strength is not comparable with that one of a fist or a palm, that's why they need training. It takes a lot of time and it is difficult to get success. But if your have strong spirit and train yourself for a long time without intervals, one of the days will bring you success. If after successful acquirement of the exercise you strike the enemy with your fingers, you can inflict a severe wound to him and if you strike with force, you can kill him. That exercise has direct resemblance to such exercises from the section "Deadly Arm" as "Saddle" (MA AN GONG) and "Palm of Guanyin[67]" (GUANYIN ZHANG)[68].

_____

Editor's notes:

[66] ZHEN JIU, Acupuncture, traditional method of the Chinese medicine which uses needles and cautery for curing diseases.

[67] GUANYIN, the Goddess of Mercy in Buddhism (AVALOKITESVARA).

[68] See for detail: Jin Jing Zhong. Training Methods of 72 Arts of Shaolin. Tanjin, 1934.

At the first training stage of the exercise "Pinching a flower" you need not to use any supporting means, you need only to closely put the forefinger and the middle finger together and press on them with your thumb. All three fingers come into contact together with their tips in the first phalange. Make unscrewing movements very slowly in the outside direction on a circle. Then, make certain

number of unscrewing movements in the inside directions, make after it certain number of unscrewing movements from inside to outside and so on. Number of movements to each side must be the same. For example, if rotation in the inside direction was done 100 times, rotation in the outside direction should be also done 100 times. Do it every day and do not limit number of repetition, do the exercise if you have spare time. If your fingers hurt, have a rest and then continue to do the exercise. For the present, do not use any tools, do not learn a lot of techniques at the same time. You can conduct lessens at any convenient place and time. It is not easy for a stranger to understand what you are doing, therefore the exercise is very convenient.

If you persistently train yourself during one year, the force in fingers will increase by several dozens of times. In that case you may start to use three soybeans of the biggest size, squeeze them with the thumb, the middle finger, and the forefinger as before and make rotating movements. It is practically impossible to use three beans at the same time in the beginning by turning (rolling) them between fingers, as they will fall off all the time. One can learn to do it through diligent training during one month. Continue to train yourself in the same way during one year. During that period of time, it is necessary to gradually increase time of training in pinching soybeans. Do one or two times every day in the beginning, gradually improve mastery, replace, if necessary, beans with new ones. It is necessary to reach such a condition when fingers squeeze three beans together, but do not use force at that and only rotate (roll) them with fingers. When the beans are reduced into powder, the first stage in acquirement of that kind of Gong Fu is over.

It is necessary to replace soybeans with pebbles[69] and continue training according to the same method. Try to reach by training that small pebbles may be reduced into powder by squeezing them in a pinch. Replace them later by more solid minerals[70]. It is of no importance how solid the stones are, they can be reduced into powder with fingers. That is the end of process of acquiring this kind of Gong Fu. You have to spend not less than 5 or 6 years from the beginning till full acquirement of the exercise. Training with an "empty hand" takes one year, pinching beans one more year, squeezing the "yellow stones" from half a year to two years. Training with "green stones" will take two or more years. Even if you make a progress in doing the exercise as fast as possible, it will take 5 years at least.

After successful acquirement of that Gong Fu it is of no importance how hard is a thing: you take it with fingers and break at once, nothing to say about blood vessels and muscles of (my or another man's) body. People often use fingers in everyday life and make various movements with them. When

---

Editor's notes:

[69] HUANG SHI in the original text, lit. "yellow stones", probably stones of some soft rocks.
[70] QING SHI, "green stone" in the original text, probably granite.

you reach perfection in that exercise, you can, accidentally and unwillingly, cause a body damage to a man or to some thing. Therefore, if a man exercises that kind of Gong Fu, it is necessary to use the left arm, do not use the right one. Other people and I use the left arm and comparatively few people use the right arm trying to do the least harm. One must be very careful in training and life. Those who are far from moral perfection and have not reached the sharpness of mind must not set their arms going and wounds people. It is strictly prohibited by any pugilistic school. It is possible to wound a man thoughtlessly, therefore, one needs to be extremely careful. For that reason respectful masters of Martial Arts taught people the techniques of "Deadly Arm" with reluctance, and they themselves trained only their left hand. The trainee who deeply learnt that technique must consolidate his will-power and always be exceptionally careful.

Shaolin Kung Fu Online Library
www.kungfulibrary.com

Chinese Martial Arts - Theory & Practice
Old Chinese Books, Treatises, Manuscripts

Lam Sai Wing. Moving Along the Hieroglyph Gung, I Tame the Tiger with the Pugilistic Art.

Lam Sai Wing. Tiger and Crane Double Form.

Lam Sai Wing. TID SIN: Iron Thread.

Jin Jing Zhong. Training Methods of 72 Arts of Shaolin.

Jin Jing Zhong. Dian Xue Shu: Skill of Acting on Acupoints.

Liu Jin Sheng. CHIN NA FA: Skill of Catch and Hold.

Tang Ji Ren. Pugilistic Art of the Tang Family. DA HONG QUAN.

Xu Yi Qian. CHUAN NA QUAN: Style of Piercing Blows and Holds.

Yuan Chu Cai. MEI HUA ZHUANG: Poles of Plum Blossom. External and Internal Training.

 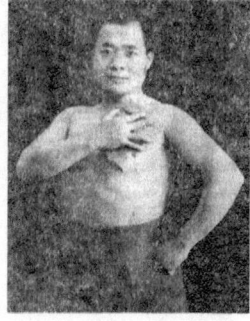